+KAOS
TEN YEARS OF
HACKING AND
MEDIA ACTIVISM
AUTISTICI/
INVENTATI

Theory on Demand #23
+KAOS. Ten Years of Hacking and Media Activism

With forewords by Maxigas, Ferry Byte, and Sandrone Dazieri.
Authors: Autistici/Inventati

Editor: Laura Beritelli
Translation: Laura Beritelli, Trish Byrne, reginazabo, blicero, and other anonymous supporters
who we are very thankful to.
Editorial Support: Miriam Rasch

Cover design: Katja van Stiphout
Design: Inga Luchs
EPUB development: Inga Luchs

Publisher: Institute of Network Cultures, Amsterdam, 2017
ISBN: 978-94-92302-16-8

English Edition, April 2017
First published in Italian as *+Kaos. 10 anni di hacking e mediattivismo*, Agenzia X, 2012.

Contact
Institute of Network Cultures
Phone: +3120 5951865
Email: info@networkcultures.org
Web: http://www.networkcultures.org

This publication is available through various print on demand services and freely downloadable
from http://networkcultures.org/publications

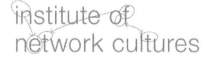

This book is dedicated to the community of our users.

CONTENTS

Prefactious by Ferry Byte 7

Preface by Maxigas 11

Introduction to the English Edition by A/I 19

Foreword by Sandrone Dazieri 21

**PART I: From 1990 to 2001
From the Panther to Genoa G8** 22

Setting the Scene, 1990-2000
Hacktivism, 1990-2000
The ECN Experience
The Greater Milan Area – Autistici
Florence – Inventati
Bologna
First Meeting
The Foundation
Online
Training
Direct Communication
Indymedia
The Joy of Doing
Hackmeeting in Catania: A Train Load of 486s
Genoa

**PART II: From 2001 to 2006
From the Genoa Aftermath to the Politics of Emergency** 71

Setting the Scene, 2001-2006
Hacktivism, 2001-2006
After Genoa 2001
European Social Forum
Kaos Tour and Communications Strategies
Legal Cases – Trenitalia, 2004
Towards Plan R*: A/I's Inadvertent Centrality
Legal Cases – Aruba Crackdown, 2004-2005
Plan R*
Download a Copy, Upload an Idea
No(b)logs

PART III: From 2006 to 2011
Recent Years or Before the World Changed   **105**

Setting the Scene, 2006-2011
Hacktivism, 2006-2011
A Collaborative Network
Legal Cases
Orwell's Grandchildren
Legal Cases – The Norwegian Crackdown
Toilet Duties by Ginox

Glossary   **126**

References   **140**

PREFACTIOUS: THE INVENTED VOICES OF A UNIQUE AND UNREPEATABLE AUTISM

Prepare yourselves to read a book where cryptography[1]-obsessed activists lay bare their organization, and the digital communication that has totally or partially accompanied your existence in recent years under the banner of media activism, literally materializes and even gets nicknamed, repeatedly.

If you are compulsive users of Autistici/Inventati's or Indymedia Italy's grassroots servers, this is the right place to figure out the mechanics that underlie the Italian media activists' digital communications. The unveiling of these mechanics will surprise you, but most of all, it will necessarily change you and allow your consciences to evolve (from the current state of things), thus impacting upon your perception of how the world, not only the digital, works.

This book has been surprising to me, who belongs neither to Autistici and Inventati's generation nor crew, but consider myself – genealogically and ideally – their elder brother. After the preface I wrote about *Mela Marcia*,[2] I welcome the opportunity of writing a new, factious preface, or a prefactious. In fact, you have to be *partly* a *partisan* if you want to fully appreciate this book, whose merits include the ability to turn the greater *part* of the people who decide to read this book into *partisans*, even if they are not fans of Italian media activism. One of the worthiest aspects of this book is its narrative approach, revealing the real nature of the relationship between politics and media (be they digital or not), between real powers and temporary forms of counterpower.

I gobbled up this book; its narrative literally overwhelmed me – a wild stream of voices tracing back a decade-long history of passion and rage, gaffes and ideas. These feelings characterized the activities of a large collective of digital activists who became talked about the world over. The greatest merit of this choral story – a virtual transcription of many oral underground subcultures that have emerged like an underground river – is its ability to humanize a certain kind of digital communication; knowing that behind a service, an acronym, a blogging platform, an anonymous remailer, there is a certain nickname, a person in flesh and blood – with her character, gender, age, and opinions – certainly adds an extra value to what we have enjoyed through our laptop screens during these long, hard years.

Hard, that's what they were – hard, painful, and demanding. That's how they appear in this book, and that's how they should be described by someone who has had the will and resolution to talk on the web about an Italian movement that in the last few years has witnessed killings, arrests, and jail, as though a revolution had exploded or a ghost was haunting the world... But the voices of the movement against the high speed train or of the anti-globalization protests deserve(d) a lot more attention, also in view of the latest developments and especially of the policies – often unreasonable and socially useless – these struggles try to resist.

---

1   Please refer to the glossary at the end.
2   *Mela Marcia*: 'Rotten Apple', a collectively authored critical history of Apple Inc., published by Agenzia X in Milan. Collettivo NGN, *Mela Marcia*, Milano: Agenzia X, 2010.

Over ten years these folks have had to face the G8 and the TAV, as well as the fierce attack by the recording industry and the Italian copyright enforcement agency against the free sharing of information online. During this decade businesses and political organizations have reacted with violence to counter-information[3] efforts they found offensive. There has been a series of trials and server seizures. Privacy has melted like snow in the face of Facebook's sun, and our digital lives have been swept away by the tsunami of globalization, by the airbus of the financial crisis. Our world has been devastated in just one decade. So don't be astonished if you see them in their dark clothes, with their suspicious gazes and their sharp tongues. They've kept their crude, direct style in order to stay focused during these hard, challenging years.

But the underlying tone of this book does not carry a sense of sadness, nostalgia, or defeat. What prevails throughout the whole story is humor, a good friend of cleverness and critique. This is actually the last resource we can use to survive under siege, when we feel the techno-control breathing down our neck… They're watching us, even if we've only set up a network of encrypted communications for food recipes!

This book is full of stories, but it also leaves a lot untold. Perhaps this is the important part of its fundamental message: while motivations and justifications are often hard to explain, the guiding thread is extremely sober – it is made of reflections and actions which are undeniably aimed towards a notion of common good, and of improvement of individual and collective perspectives. The red thread of this book is the movements that fight for an alternative to the current state of affairs.

As you read this book, you will hear the hissing of *The Matrix* in the background – the parallel history of the technical evolution of online communication, as seen from the uncomfortable vantage point of a willing, self-declared avant-garde. Having had the opportunity of experimenting with a range of technological potentialities for the first time, these people enjoyed the privilege of turning into high-tech Cassandras, of saying repeatedly 'I told you so!' to smaller or larger audiences who were mostly reluctant to understand and challenge the latest developments.

In a handful of years, we went from listening to night time radio transmissions of weird sounds like bzz… scrthcchh… ftbleehh…, recording them on audio tapes (!?!) to be properly modulated and demodulated (wow! that's what the name 'modem' comes from!), and using them as software for our friend's ZX Spectrum (because he was the only one who could afford to buy it), to the wonders of the social-networked world. But in between there were the bulletin board systems (BBSs), the birth of the web, newsgroups, Internet-relay chat (IRC) channels, mailing lists, email, blogs, online videos, and all the social media… A decade seen through

---

3   Counter-information: A term commonly used in 1970s in Italy to describe responses to the censored or distorted versions of events published in the mainstream media. This alternative press encompassed both activist publishers and investigative journalists lifting the lid on the shady incidents. These efforts were especially significant amidst the so-called 'strategy of tension' – bombings orchestrated by sectors of the state, carried out by the far right, and used to justify repression of the left – and in specific incidents such as the death of the anarchist Pinelli through defenestration. The concept of counter-information has been superseded by that of 'alternative media', but is arguably best understood as both a product of media history (the period where news and information was still highly centralized, especially in the case of TV) and a moment in the history of ideas, where it was believed that if only people knew the truth they could, and would, act to change society. The term is still used today but usually in a more casual manner.

the multiple lenses of a collective engaged in counter-information about the most diverse and extreme situations. This has created a host of tech-savvy people who are now facing (until the next generation appears) who knows how many new adversities and technical innovations at the same time. A/I means Autistici/Inventati, but it could just as easily refer to artificial intelligence. At any rate, temporary autonomous zones (TAZ) are still very much needed, and tools for online communication will still be useful in the future, without distracting our attention from reflecting on the contents and ideas that need to be disseminated.

Ferry Byte

PREFACE

The memories and reflections in the next chapters capture ten years of hacking and media activism by Autistici/Inventati, as well as a taste of bad-ass Italian underground attitude – but I try to show that they do so much more. As an activist collective taking care of social movements' data, A/I effectively soaked up much of the repression by the state and capital against the subversive political elements of the extra-parliamentary radical left. No matter if the authorities targeted anti-capitalist (in Genoa), anti-prison (Black Cross), anti-industrial (No TAV), or anti-clerical (Molleindustria) groups, went for specific individuals, well chosen informal collectives, particular registered organizations or grassroots social movements in general, they had to cross ways with A/I. Therefore, the story of A/I is the story of political struggles of the extra-parliamentary left, seen from close proximity to (sometimes smashed) computer screens.

Hacking emerged as one of the most prolific areas of grassroots struggles around the turn of the millennium. Cyberpunk imaginaries fuelled the belief that if marginalized people master networking techniques faster than the state and capital, then they can outpace or outlive the powers that be. Such reading persisted in the radical imagination despite the fact that narratives of cyberpunk dystopias rarely end well. As the revolutionary Autonomist movements – firmly rooted in Italy – ran out of steam, a desperate retreat to the Temporary Autonomous Zones of Hakim Bey ensued. Cyberspace was the most concrete and most powerful manifestation of such a zone, which capitalism had not yet fully penetrated. Chaos theory – enthusiastically received by hackers as an almost metaphysical world view – provided an antidote to another popular idea: social order as an all-encompassing self-regulating 'system', without an outside and without any chance for subversion.

While the cyberpunk experience may seem naive in hindsight, it was the lived reality of the era. Following the burst of the dot-com bubble, it took capital a decade more to recuperate cyberspace as a medium of capital accumulation and workers' exploitation. When states finally colonized networks yet another decade later, the other foot came down: the internet solidified as a cutting-edge instrument of surveillance and repression. Thus, radical technology collectives such as A/I grew out of a historical moment when users' appropriation of technologies outpaced the integration of those technologies into systemic requirements.

Radical Technology Collectives

Radical technology collectives (hereafter RTCs) provide online infrastructures like mailboxes and websites to mostly local activist groups and individuals. RTCs are usually territorial in the sense that they mainly collaborate with activists in a given city, region, country or movement. Positioned at a passage point where social conflicts are translated between political, technical and legal matters, A/I have earned the trust of activists in Italy, and increasingly in other countries.

A/I was forged in the heat of the alter-globalization cycle of struggles and played a significant part in the movement. Unlike many other activist groups such as Indymedia, they have continued to be active to this day. Moreover, they persisted in the new strategic context of increased (awareness of) mass surveillance. In contrast, some commercial providers with a similar profile such as Lavabit (that Edward Snowden used) and Silent Circle (associated with security expert Phil Zimmermann) closed down in 2013 in response to pressure from author-ities. Meantime, hackers and startups churned out a whole range of software in response to the situation, most of which promised users delivery from surveillance by simply installing an app. None of these solutions achieved notable uptake.

Ultimately, the problem with commercial offers and decentralized software applications boils down to the same thing. In order to challenge state repression and capitalist exploitation effectively, it is necessary to stand and organize collectively against the state and capital. Cypherpunk initiatives like Lavabit or decentralized software can go a long way to challenge the status quo, but they are historically limited by their understanding of social change and social conflict.

Social change is not simply a matter of consumer preference like the choice of an individual's email provider, neither social conflicts are mere mathematical problems that can be resolved through a strategic application of mathematics. Radical technology collectives build political solidarity and nurture security behaviors within and between activist groups in addition to providing things like email and putting the right cryptographic algorithms in place.

Maintenance and Repair

Even though the actual everyday practice of hacktivism is mostly about maintenance, groups that run infrastructure have received little to zero attention so far. This is especially ironic because even the emblematic movement of contemporary hacktivism (Anonymous) could not operate without relying on the services of radical server collectives. While it is the spec-tacular acts of disruption that go down in history, the daily labor of infrastructure maintenance makes history to a comparable degree. Therefore, it is necessary to rethink the history of technological resistance from a use-centric point of view in order to counterbalance innova-tion-centric narratives.

RTCs such as A/I are not famous for their role in advancing the state of the art in cryptography, or proposing a new relationship to their customers such as Lavabit. They are well-known for the correct implementation of mainstream security best practices and for fixing widely-used broken software when it exposes its users to risks. Their main objective is the stable and sustainable operation of services based on mutual aid and solidarity. These are values that no social contract or technical contraption can guarantee. While the strength of Anons lies in their unpredictable actions and their obscure identities, users of RTCs benefit from reliable responses to situations and the street credibility of operators. Arguably, all these are equally important in the context of a strategy based on the diversity of tactics. Why is then that the contributions of activist who build, maintain and repair information infrastructures are gen-erally less recognized?

The primary reason is a strong bias towards invention in accounts of hacktivism, which stems from the modern myth that technological progress goes hand in hand with social progress – and the equally misleading notion that historical shifts are caused by the appearance of new ideas. In fact, the history and sociology of technology holds a vast warehouse of examples where more efficient techniques or more progressive ideas failed to take root in the techno-logical landscape or in the social fabric. Implementation, maintenance and repair is just as important for changing society – or even just technology – as innovation.

The secondary – and more prosaic – reason is that infrastructural labor is often the kind of 'backstage' work that is rarely noticed, discussed or credited simply because it happens behind the scenes. While A/I probably supported a myriad of spectacular direct actions through providing a trusted platform for undercover organizing, they do not necessarily appear as actors themselves in the specific conflict. Anons often rally around activist causes by shutting down websites, disclosing documents or simply publishing threats. However, they tend to move with the self-righteousness of superheroes, without much deference to the street level movements they claim to side with – or the hacktivists who maintain the infrastructure that they sometimes rely on.

All in all, the role of RTCs in social movements is under-documented and under-theorized because it is neither innovative nor spectacular. Yet, the historical record shows that it is a more effective way to address rampart problems of state surveillance, democratic deficit and capitalist exploitation than what more publicized startup companies or software projects can come up with. Apart from being a privileged lens for a long view of grassroots struggles in Italy, it is also for this reason that Autistici/Inventati's story is a worthy read.

European Circuits of Hacking

It may not be apparent at first sight, but it is a crucial fact that European hacking scenes are organized into somewhat isolated circuits on a territorial basis. I argue that there are at least three larger circuits that can be identified, tied to the geographical regions of Central Europe, Western Europe, and Southern Europe. This partly explains why so few participants and observers from the hegemonic Western European countries are aware of the legendary A/I experience, or why it might look irrelevant to those who are familiar with it.

However, before dwelling on the distinctions between the European circuits of hacking, it may be useful to clarify the concept of the scene. A scene is mainly comprised of places, communication platforms and periodic gatherings. Participants agree on where to cultivate their passion locally, how to keep in touch with each other, and when they all meet in person. The latter are periodic rituals where members gather to experience the scene in its most essential form. Hacker anthropologist Gabriella Coleman notes that the hacker convention is the material condensation of everything that is important to hackers. The idea of the scene allows us to understand hacker culture not as an abstract generalization, but as an empirical reality of bodies and machines performing concrete functions. Some would presume – wrongly – that the scene is an ideal-typical unit of analysis that refers to a number of family resemblances, as 'geek' does in the works of Christopher Kelty, another seminal anthropologist of hacker culture. Scenes understand themselves as scenes and articulate themselves in well defined – yet idiosyncratic – forms. Others would criticize the notion of the scene as a nostalgic reference to an ideal community characterized by bucolic harmony and unified ideology. On the contrary, a scene provides the very context in which participants collectively experience, negotiate, and struggle over the meaning of their favorite activities.

Central Europe (Scandinavia, parts of Eastern Europe, and Germany) nourished the demoscene, focused on producing demos: audio-visual demonstrations of computer capabilities. Demos were shown and judged in a competitive way at demoscene parties. Common criteria were aesthetic appeal (graphics, sound, design, direction) and technical innovation (special effects, algorithmic elegance, executable size). Both were evaluated relative to the architectural platform used (such as ZX Spectrum, Commodore 64, or later IBM PC). Since the 1990s, sceners organized themselves into production groups modelled after the already popular cracking groups that released pirated software. They typically came together at friends' homes to work and communicated with each other through diskmags and later BBSs (Bulletin Board Systems). While anarchist themed demos were common at parties, the scene was barely politicized beyond an anti-authoritarian ethos. A relevant example is the case of tomcat, who played a significant role in the internationally renowned Hungarian demoscene, and even wrote one of the few book-length works on the topic.[4] He reappeared a decade later as a prankster associated with extreme right groups.

Western Europe established its hacker scene almost simultaneously with the hegemonic United States. In 1984 the icons immortalized by Levy[5] met in California at the invitation of Steward Brand,[6] editor of the *Whole Earth Catalog* (an emblematic countercultural encyclopedia of the era) at what was termed the first Hackers Conference. The same year the Chaos Computer Club held its first Chaos Communication Congress in Hamburg, Germany.[7] While the former became an invitation-only old boys' club, the latter developed into the major meeting point of hackers in the continent. Security research is the main focus of this stream of hacker culture, and at least some of its founders – such as Wau Holland – are strongly associated with the radical left. Therefore, it is no wonder that they met repression early on. In response, they built legitimacy for hacking as a form of public education, policy advocacy and consumer protection. Coleman and Golub[8] are spot-on here when they point out (in connection with the US context) that repression was an important factor in the institutionalization of the scene. By the end of the 1990s, the CCC was a consultative expert body to the German constitutional court. Hackers met regularly in legally established hackerspaces to socialize, learn collaboratively, as well as to work on technical projects individually or together. Hackerspaces developed beyond associations of the local CCC chapters to an explosive global phenomenon.[9]

Southern European hackers began to organize publicly only in the late 1990s. Hacker culture did not encounter a strong state or a hegemonic computer industry that could have forced it underground, into the market or into the confines of civil society institutions. Instead, hackers could develop their own meanings more autonomously, while inspired by local political movements. In contrast to Western Europe, in the South it was not the highly visible groups but the annual meetings that came first. The first hackmeeting took place in Florence (1998), while the Iberian peninsula followed suit with its own hackmeeting in Barcelona (2000). The Milan hackmeeting (1999) ended with a discussion about hacklabs like the one in Catania, Sicily (founded in 1995). Participants reached a common agreement and a collective desire to establish similar shared machine shops in their native cities. Since many of them lived or worked in occupied social centers, they often had the real estate covered. In a few years, many

---

4   Polgár Tamás, *Freax: The History of the Computer Demoscene*, Winnenden: CSW-Verlag, 2005.
5   Steven Levy, *Hackers: Heroes of the Computer Revolution*, Garden City, NY: Anchor Press, Doubleday, 1984.
6   Fred Turner, *From Counterculture to Cyberculture: Stewart Brand, the Whole Earth Network, and the Rise of Digital Utopianism*, Chicago, IL: University of Chicago Press, 2006.
7   Daniel Kulla, *Der Phrasenprüfer: Szenen aus dem Leben von Wau Holland, Mitbegründer Des Chaos-Computer-Clubs* [the Voltage Tester – Scenes from the Life of Wau Holland, Co-Founder of the Chaos Computer Club], Birkenau-Löhrbach: Werner Pieper & The Grüne Kraft, 2003.
8   Gabriella Coleman and Alex Golub, 'Hacker Practice: Moral Genres and the Cultural Articulation of Liberalism', *Anthropological Theory* 8.3 (September, 2008): 255-277.
9   Bre and Astera (eds) *Hackerspaces: The Beginning*, 2008. Available at: http://blog.hackerspaces. org/2011/08/31/hackerspaces-the-beginning-the-book/.

well-known Italian squats added hacklabs to the usual assortment of infoshops, freeshops, soup kitchens, and concert halls. Hacklabs became the meeting places of hackers and at the same time an indispensable part of the anarchist movements' repertoire.[10] As the A/I story demonstrates, activities included developing free software and building computers from recycled hardware, setting up classrooms and teaching activists and immigrants, as well as fulfilling the infrastructural needs of media activists. Just like with the hackmeeting tradition, hacklab founders in Spain were inspired by the Italian experience.

As evident from this description, hacking here was not simply politically conscious (as in the North), but actually integrated with grassroots social movements. While in his classic work on the connection between countercultures and cybercultures – which established the 'edge' of US hacking – Fred Turner had to painstakingly piece together the ideological and political connections between the two, in the case of Austistici/Inventati the link is so blatantly obvious that it is impossible to discuss hacking without street level political action. The subsequent chapters of this book testify to it.

All in all, the basic structure of these scenes closely resemble each other, down to the count-er-intuitive fact that in order to understand the virtual reality-obsessed hacker culture, one has to pay close attention to the materiality of the urban environment, the affective meetings of bodies, and the local contexts of social history.

Nonetheless, Central European demosceners go to parties (which are on the edge of extinc-tion), Western European hackers go to Congresses, and Southern European hackers attend hackmeetings. Tellingly, participants of one circuit are often aware and sometimes even attend the annual meetings of other circuits. Yet, they do not feel at home in the spaces of other circuits. They find it hard to identify with adjacent hacker scenes. Therefore, it seems that hacking in Europe is constituted as a series of overlapping but mostly isolated circuits, which do not provide a single identity to participants.

Attempts at Bridge Building

Of course, there have been efforts to bridge the gap. In fact, the argument for understanding European hacking as a series of circuits is supported by examining the consistent failures of bringing them together. At the same time, bridge building efforts also show that the reality is more complicated than the schematic categories loosely proposed above. Hacklabs could be found as far up North as Scandinavia, the decisive moment in the experience of hack-erspaces was its appropriation by US hackers, and the demoscene was arguably started in the Netherlands. Still, these broad categories may be still able to capture something of the statistical veracity and the socio-cultural texture of hacking in various territories.

The Connect Congress of the Plug'n'Politix network happened twice (2001, Zürich, Egocity squat; 2004, Barcelona, Camorra & Cyber*forat squats) as a meeting gathering 'open-access spaces, anarchist computing collectives, and hacklabs'.[11] The phrasing makes clear what

---

10   Maxigas, *Peer Production of Open Hardware: Unfinished Artefacts and Architectures in the Hackerspaces*, PhD diss., Barcelona: Internet Interdisciplinary Institute/Open University of Catalunya, 2015.

11   darkveggy, 'Invitation to "Connect Congress 2004" in BCN', posting to the hacklabs mailing list, 13 October 2004, https://listas.sindominio.net/pipermail/hacklabs/2004-October/000608.html.

was already known to the participants: hackers will attend from Spanish and Italian hacklabs, and so will their perceived counterparts from the 'open-access spaces' (also called squatted internet cafés or simply internetworkingspaces) ASCII and PUSCII in the Netherlands (Amsterdam, Utrecht) or EgoCity in Switzerland (Zürich). It is also interesting and relevant that French hacktivists played an important part in these attempts, since hacklabs were also found there, and the two cultures hybridized. One said that 'I wanted to bring together the efficiency and solidity of organisation in the North with the all-around human connection of the South'.[12]

The TransHackMeeting (short for Transcultural Hackmeeting) was a complementary initiative that 'aims at extending the ongoing Italian and Spanish hackmeeting movement [...] to expand this beyond geographical borders'.[13] Again, a similar assortment of people attended and the experience was repeated in 2007 Oslo, as well as proposed for 2010 Istanbul as '3 days hackmeetings shaped after hk.it and hk.es, extending the movement over traditional geo. borders'.[14] The mailing list was hosted by a famous Italian Radical Technology Collective (A/I, of course).

backbone409 (2014, Calafou, near Barcelona) was rather about going beyond the hackmeeting tradition while increasing the focus on infrastructural activism, but it addressed Iberian collectives as much as the wider European radical hosting scene. Even English-Spanish simultaneous translation was provided as a response to past experiences with language barriers. Even though the Iberian peninsula may have spawned as many Radical Technology Collectives as the rest of the world combined, relatively few attended.[15]

Taken together or separately, these meetings failed to produce a tradition or initiatives of their own. They remained a transnational medium of communication between different collectives, rather than a cultural melting pot or a regional movement such as hacklabs or hackerspaces. What they did achieve was to bring together the most politically motivated from a relatively diverse palette of technical enthusiasts. It is perhaps not a coincidence that it was the political activists amongst the various streams of European hacking that tried to connect the different circuits. The English translation of +Kaos fits into these series as a small contribution towards mutual understanding and solidarity.

In the meantime, what really united these circles was also very clear from the beginning. They have all been formed through the appropriation of the imperialist US computing cultures, which became a lingua franca for the hackers of the Old Continent (where colonialism was obviously invented). As the recent collected volume Hacking Europe testifies, the common thread in the various ways that European hackers appropriated US computing cultures was a relatively higher social consciousness and closer interaction with their local political struggles. Alternative currents in society had a much more significant role to play in framing the meaning of computers than in the United States. Possible explanations include the weaker presence of national capital and a more supportive policy environment defined by national

12   Interview with darkveggy, 20 March 2014.
13   Montaparadiso Hacklab wiki contributors, 'Transnational Hackmeeting', 2004, http://web.archive.org/
      web/20040607030557/http://twiki.fazan.org/bin/view/Transhackmeeting.
14   transhackmeeting.org, '(Un)hack the Bosphorus: TransHackMeeting Istanbul 2010', Slides from the
      HackerSpaceFestival, /tmp/lab near Paris, France, 2009, http://sandbox.benn.org/sli/hsf2009/thk2010_
      hsf2009.pdf.
15   backbone409 organizers, 'Backbone409: Participants', 2014, https://backbone409.calafou.org.

states. Unfortunately, these alternative takes on the social meaning – and political purpose – of computers largely subsided as European computing cultures were integrated into the global flow of capital.

Laboratory Italy

In the introduction of a seminal English language collection on the 1970s Autonomia cycle of struggles, Michael Hardt refers to the idea of the Italian laboratory.[16] The argument is that given its exceptionally strong social movements and its relative isolation from other European countries, the Italian experience is both idiosyncratic and exemplary. Reproducing it without its wider socio-historical context is impossible, while at the same time it offers valuable lessons to consider elsewhere.

Even though falling for stereotypes is a very real possibility in such an assessment, something remains to be said about the character of the national scene in which A/I was a visible player. It is no doubt that Italian hackers produced the most vibrant expression of political cyberpunk, as a kind of the West Coast version of the European take on hacking. The critique of instrumental reason embodied in the corporate version of computing was deeply ingrained in the political wing of each circuit (and each scene had its political wing). Nonetheless, there were crucial differences of perspectives and urgencies. In terms of audience, Northern hackers focused their attention on the general public, while Southern hackers communicated more closely with the social movements. The different strategies made sense as far as Southern social movements actually had a connection with the wider population and a stronger role to play in politics. In terms of computing, Northern hackers' interest was captivated by producing results through technical means, while the South seized on the opportunity to realize an experience in line with George Sorel's understanding of the General Strike as a mobilizing myth: the computer as the engine of the revolution.

If one region focused on computers and networks as a security apparatus and the other as a medium, maybe differences can be accounted for by their roles in the global division of labor. Core economies tend to possess more balanced media and a more competent secret service, while half-peripheral ones more propagandistic media and a more under-resourced secret service. Yet Italy was surely a regional center in the context of Southern Europe: both hacklabs and hackmeetings emerged from the squatting and anarchist scene there and spread to the adjacent Iberian peninsula and to a lesser extent Greece and even France.

Meanwhile, it would be a mistake to underestimate the significance of cultural factors in shaping the expression of social conflict and electronic resistance. Tatiana Bazzichelli argues that cyberpunk was a political movement only in Italy, largely thanks to the context created by the Decoder group and magazine established in 1987.[17] This wider cultural appeal must have helped to make A/I the largest political hacker group on the continent in terms of core membership, despite the fact that admission criteria are strict, including a long track record of mutual affinity and personal trust between administrators.

---

16 Michael Hardt, 'Introduction: Laboratory Italy', in Michael Hardt and Paolo Virno (eds) *Radical Thought in Italy: A Potential Politics*, Minnesota: University of Minnesota Press, 1996, 1-10.
17 Tatiana Bazzichelli, *Networking: The Net as Artwork*, Aarhus: Digital Aesthetics Research Center, Aarhus University, 2009.

Perhaps more than its bigger brother (the Riseup collective), A/I represents a captivating idea of what the Radical Technology Collectives as a movement in particular and computing in general can be in the beginning of the 21st century. More than a grand vision, however, it is a desperate attempt to rescue humanity from the onslaught of social decline brought about by the development of capitalist technologies, articulating the conflicts that converge on cybernetic infrastructures. A/I's Noblogs farm sports a Ballard quote to this effect: 'The environment is so full of television, party political broadcasts and advertising campaigns that you hardly need to do anything.'.

Maxigas

INTRODUCTION TO THE ENGLISH EDITION: A STORY INSIDE THE STORY

We're the Italian collective Autistici/Inventati, better known as simply Autistici, or A/I. We are a radical left political collective promoting online communication privacy and anonymity. The collective was formed in 2001. In 2011 we thought that it would be wise to get an account of this experience down in writing, before bits got lost and memories mixed up. So we wrote this book to celebrate our 10th anniversary. We printed it, and started distributing it in June 2012 in collaboration with the independent Italian publisher AgenziaX.

The book was meant to tell our story, but ended up describing the peculiar relationship between hacktivism and activism, in Italy and beyond. It turned out to be a testimony of sorts. Since its publication, many have been asking for an English translation. This is it, appearing nearly five years after the Italian edition and more than fifteen years after A/I was founded, with a German and a Spanish translation also under way.

We hope that the story of a collective as seen from inside can offer a useful stimulus to others who find themselves amidst similar dynamics, not exactly as an example to be emulated, but rather as a case study in misfortune, enthusiasm, disappointment, success, errors, laughter, exhaustion, and so on, through the whole plethora of incidents and relationships encountered by a group such as our own.

The text is basically divided into three parts: the birth of the collective, its activity up until 2006, and its activity from then until around 2010. The book is primarily composed of interviews because none of us would ever have had either the desire or time to piece these ten years back together. The idea and the opportunity arose when Laura proposed to us to interview someone from the collective to tell the story of its birth, and thus the book was born, from interviews made by Laura and others. Laura's drafts were then reviewed and supplemented by the rest of the group, resulting in a work which is to some degree an artifice of many authors, and a hybrid between self-documentation and an outline of events in chronological order.

One of the main problems we had to confront was whom to interview. Over the years dozens of people have been involved in A/I. To speak with everyone would have taken too long, and run the risk of remaining forever unfinished. Thus a conscious decision was made to be partial, beginning with whoever was still in the collective and had the desire to tell the story. Then we moved on to those who had left but with whom we were still in touch, or those who were easier to track down. And then we stopped, knowing that the resulting work might be incomplete.

But better incomplete than unfinished, and in any case we needed an excuse to do another book in 2020. Wherever interviews reference events, or episodes which could be confusing to those not present, we have tried to provide the context at the start of the relevant section. In addition we have added references to the text and attached a short glossary at the end. Words in the glossary are highlighted in the text, such that should the reader dip in and out of the text, explanations for more obscure terms are available.

The final English edition is the result of a collaboration among people from within the community, both Italian and English native speakers. They collected, reviewed, and edited each other's work. It's still rough on the edges, but we thought it was time to start sharing it.

Someone said the digital world has changed during these last five years. Surely, the common understanding of it has – and that has had an impact on A/I too. We are primarily a community though, and we r*esist. We promise however to write all about it on our 20th anniversary.

This book is dedicated to our users, because ultimately we are here for them, a small community of crazy and generous people.

A/I collective,

June 2015

FOREWORD

On the A32 highway, the police are trying to break through the No TAV[18] blockade for the third time. The air is heavy with truncheon blows and stones, and the first rows of the Valsusa inhabitants are already being hit in the face with riot shields; it's lucky that they are defensive instruments. The noise of smashed teeth reaches all the way to where I am, a ways back, smoking a cigarette which tastes like tear gas. On the fourth attack, the perimeter of the road block is broken. The demonstrators fan out as the line of riot police penetrates the crowd like a knife: the roll of the batons sounds like machine-gun fire. During the ensuing flight a small group of No TAV protesters stays behind and stops near my position: the hard core, ready to resist until the end. No, I look more carefully – average age: 60. The oldest are slow runners. I get closer. An old lady is propping up a young man, injured? No, I hear them talking.

'A bit unfit, ain't you, boy? We've run for forty meters and they haven't taken out the water cannons yet.'

'Madam, I can't anymore. Leave me here, I'll chain myself to the guardrail.' After which he hugs the road protections like a koala.

We are a few steps apart. I see his face and he sees mine. 'Goril...!' he cries with broken voice. I recognize him, it's Malaussene. When I was at Leoncavallo[19] he was always hacking computers and talked like a pod person from Mars. A hacker, a nerd. I tell him to get up and follow the lady, that a squad of cops is coming this way. He shakes his head and pants: 'We've written a book! I've got the draft with me.' I ask him how this can be relevant just now. He answers that if he gets caught, he will throw it towards the Tg3[20] news crew. 'The world needs to know. They must learn about our fight for the freedom of networks, for the distribution of uncensored information, the free exchange of knowledge, free software...'

The poor guy is raving. The riot police are on him now. They grab him by his feet and carry him away like a sack of potatoes. 'Gorilla', he shouts again, just before the blows subdue him. 'If we finish our book, you must write a preface. Promise me!'

'If you're still alive', I answer.

He is alive. This is the book. Enjoy it.

Sandrone Dazieri

---

18 No TAV: The movement against the high-speed train system Treno Alta Velocità (TAV) began in the early 90s in opposition to the construction of a new line from Turin through the Alps to Lyon in France. This mega project is partially funded by the European Union and has been criticized on social and environmental grounds. The struggle against the TAV widened from 2005 onwards and has become a cause célèbre.

19 Leoncavallo: Social center in Milan founded in 1975 and now in its third location. Leoncavallo developed a national profile due to the intensity of police efforts to destroy it and the determination of its occupants to defend it by any means necessary.

20 Tg3: The daily news program broadcast on RAI3; a public TV channel traditionally considered to have a leftist slant, having historically been controlled by the Communist Party (PCI).

PART 1: FROM 1990 TO 2001
FROM THE PANTHER TO GENOA G8

Setting the Scene, 1990-2000

Telling or reading a story takes imagination, but first of all one has to choose a place or an episode from which to start. To frame the historical context in which the A/I collective was born and developed we decided to begin a decade earlier in 1990, when the majority of the founders were either adolescents or just a little older. If you were not lucky enough to have been young in those years, and wish to experience the atmosphere of the times, we recommend a film: *La Guerra degli Antò*, by Riccardo Milani. Set in 1990, the film tells the story of four punks from Montesilvano (in Abruzzo, a remote Italian region) who struggle with the boredom and depression of daily life, emigrate and try and make a life for themselves, fail and return to their village.

During this period, in Italy, Andreotti's[21] sixth government was limping along, and these were the final years of the so-called *pentapartito* – the five-party coalition which had governed the Bel Paese for the whole of the 80s.[22] The Tangentopoli[23] investigation and Bettino Craxi's[24] exile marked the end of the First Republic and the beginning of the Second, which itself is coming to an end as we write, or perhaps has effectively been over for some time (although ultimately, these are changes of little importance to the people mentioned in this book, who tend to have rather stormy relationships with the state irrespective of any changes in leadership).

Following the 1990 invasion of Kuwait by Iraq, an alliance of thirty-five countries led by the US launched the first Gulf War. Meanwhile in Italy there were official revelations about Gladio, an underground anti-Soviet structure groomed by NATO and active in the country from 1956.[25]

---

21   Giulio Andreotti: Longtime leader of the Christian Democrat Party, seven-time prime minister of Italy.
22   The *pentapartito*, or five-party coalition: Christian Democrats (DC), Italian Socialist Party (PSI), Italian Social Democrat Party (PSDI), Italian Republican Party (PRI), Italian Liberal Party (PLI).
23   Tangentopoli (Bribesville): In February 1992 Italy was convulsed by revelations arising out of a judicial investigation into the payment of bribes. This began in Milan but later spread throughout the country and involved thousands of politicians. The political consequences were devastating for the major parties: the PSI was decimated and disappeared; the DC lost huge numbers of voters. The collapse of these forces cleared the way both for the growth of the racist/separatist Northern League (Lega Nord) and the entry into politics of Silvio Berlusconi in time for the 1994 election. Meanwhile the Communist Party (the biggest in western Europe) was going through its own crisis following the end of the Soviet Bloc, and split in 1991. The majority faction became the Democratic Party of the Left (later the Democratic Party, PD), whereas the minority established Communist Refoundation (PRC).
24   Bettino Craxi: Former leader of the Socialist Party and prime minister from 1983 to 1987. Craxi was charged with corruption during Tangentopoli and fled to Tunisia in 1994 to escape prosecution.
25   Gladio: NATO operation initially conceived as a contingency in the case of Europe 'going red' in the aftermath of WW2; the strength of Communist Parties in countries such as Italy and France made electoral victory seem plausible. Gladio became a key site for anti-communist networking and subversive activity on the part of state assets in collaboration with right wing militants.

Halfway through the 90s, the first Berlusconi[26] government came to power but fell after just a year; in 1999 the first D'Alema[27] government gave its blessing to armed intervention in Kosovo, so the decade opened with one war and closed with another.

On the economic front, the massive restructuring of the 1980s came to a close, destroying the centrality of the factory in the cities of the West. What emerged was a process of outsourcing production and the financialization of markets, commonly referred to as globalization. For many of us the most immediate result was an adolescence spent in areas where residential neighborhoods bordered former industrial zones – now completely abandoned.

But this outline of the major media events of those years is intended only to provide some context. Our objective is to convey the environment and atmosphere which shaped those interviewed in this book. To do so we must set aside power politics, macroeconomics and geopolitics; instead we must take to the streets of Italian cities, amid the social movements, demonstrations, and occupations. This is a more elusive history, made up of experiences often overlooked and thus even more difficult to contextualize.

One of these experiences occurred one freezing cold winter, when someone mistook a large black cat for a panther. After a police patrol confirmed the sighting a media frenzy exploded, setting off a hunt for the feline which eventually fizzled out. This is how the student movement against the Ruberti reform[28] found a name and a symbol. The Panther movement occupied numerous universities throughout 1990, and soon after the squares were filled with protests against the war in Iraq.[29] Meanwhile, self-managed spaces, squats, and occupied social centers[30] blossomed throughout the peninsula.

---

26 Silvio Berlusconi: Former cruise-ship entertainer and prime minister. The media tycoon has been convicted of tax fraud.
27 Massimo D'Alema: One-time national secretary of the Democratic Party of the Left (PDS), and prime minister from 1998 to 2000.
28 Ruberti reform: Antonio Ruberti was minister for universities and research in the years 1989-92. In 1990 he introduced a legislative reform of universities which was widely opposed. At the level of the university administration, the legislation limited student representatives to a consultative role. It also opened universities up to private financing, a step which was opposed on the grounds that it would privilege science-oriented and larger schools and lead to the effective demotion of smaller and more humanist-oriented institutions. Eventually the Pantera movement against the reform dissipated without stopping the proposed changes, but in the meantime it functioned as the incubation chamber for a revitalized political and cultural opposition.
29 The war in Iraq (1990-1991): In August 1990 Iraq invaded Kuwait. Over the next four months the US assembled a coalition of supporters and war began on the 17 January 1991. The Iraqis quickly retreated and on the 24 February US troops and their allies entered Iraq. The Iraqi army suffered significant casualties in retreat and the US declared a ceasefire on the 28 February.
30 Self-managed social centers, or *Centri sociali occupati e autogestiti* (CSOA): Since the 1970s groups of young people have squatted buildings in cities and towns to use for a combination of political, social and cultural purposes. While the type of activities varies enormously in character, there is always a bar, a concert venue and a space for meetings. The structures occupied are usually former industrial spaces and are managed by the occupants directly through weekly meetings. These occupations naturally generate conflict with the local authorities and are frequently evicted by the police. In some cases the ability of the CSOA to mobilize political and popular support leads to the assignment of an unused space by the local council; these are referred to as CSA, *Centri sociali autogestiti*. The willingness to negotiate such arrangements varies on a case-by-case basis depending on the political flavor of the

Since A/I's members emerged from such developments, attracted by the possibilities of these spaces, we will look at self-managed spaces in more detail.

In Milan, 1989, there was an attempted eviction of the self-managed social center Leoncavallo: the occupiers resisted from the roof, throwing everything possible at those besieging them below. A poster from this time remains an icon, on it is a photo of three people wielding stones and a Molotov cocktail, with the caption: 'Whatever It Takes'. Among the movements connected to the social centers there was a sense of emerging from the dark days of the 1980s. Then, on the 10 September 1994, a demonstration of the so-called Social Opposition[31] was held with the aim of protecting Leoncavallo from eviction and defending the practice of squatting more generally. The majority of the Italian social centers and many other grassroots organizations took part. Part of the reporting from independent radio from the day has become legendary in the history of alternative media. As the demonstration broke through into Via Cavour the correspondent exclaimed: 'The police are retreating, under a hail of blows the police are retreating!' This hadn't happened for years, and it wasn't to happen often in the years to come.

We do not want to encourage the misunderstanding that Leoncavallo is the epitome and inspiration behind every Italian social center: some experiences link to the long wave of *Autonomia Operaia*[32] (dating back to the 70s), others are tied to the Marxist-Leninist[33] tradition, and some have anarchist or libertarian roots.[34] All of the social centers, however, were heavily influenced by the music scene, and a subcultural sensibility. In the 80s, for example, punk was everywhere in the social centers. The experience of the Virus social center in Milan is indicative and symbolic of this fusion. Then in the 90s the mainstream media designated the social centers as the home of hip hop, and some years later came the advent of electronic music and rave parties. Bredaoccupata 3337, or Breda, one of the self-managed spaces referenced in the interviews that follow, was evicted in 1999. It was one of the first groups in the Milan area to make massive use of illegal raves in an explicitly political and confrontational manner. To do so it often left its own space and took over abandoned industrial zones.

Interest in this type of subculture was accompanied by a reflection on new media and the internet, and a fascination with cyberpunk. For example, when Breda was occupied in 1997, one of its constituent parts was the antimuzak front, a collective which organized illegal raves

---

occupants. Over the last forty years there has been a number of coordination structures at a national level involving some or many CSOA/CSA. These spaces have retained their importance due to a capacity to innovate that is otherwise scarce in Italy's conservative culture.

31   'Social Opposition': This was the banner under which Leoncavallo summoned supporters to protest in September 1994 following the eviction from their temporary home the previous month.

32   Workers' Autonomy, or *Autonomia Operaia*: The name broadly ascribed to a large part of the extra-parliamentary movement in Italy in the 1970s. It is generally regarded as being composed of at least two wings: those emanating from workplace committees and those involved in loosely subversive cultural activity. The use of violence was common in this political culture and this made it vulnerable to repression. As political violence escalated so did the prominence of more structured armed groups such as the Red Brigades.

33   Marxist-Leninist: In Italy this epithet usually indicates that the group or milieu retains a fondness for Maoism, Stalinism, or both.

34   Anarchist or libertarian: Italy has an entrenched and heterogeneous anarchist and left-libertarian culture comprising numerous currents whose approaches range from open agitation on social questions to sabotage.

in the greater Milan area from the mid-90s on. In the film *Decoder* [35] muzak is music played in McDonald's to influence the taste and behavior of its customers. Antimuzak was the antidote, whose sound would cause revolution to break out.

In 1998, several student collectives occupied a former cargo depot, Deposito Bulk, also known as the Bulk. The second Hackmeeting was held in this space in 1999. Evicted in 2000, the collectives occupied a new space, this time a warehouse belonging to the national electricity company, ENEL. It was in this new space that the Milanese hacklab, LOA, made its home.

It is important to grasp just how fertile that period was for the counterculture in Milan. Beyond the individual spaces already named, we can cite at least ten other squatted spaces in the city during this time: Cox18, Transiti, Garibaldi, Torchiera, Pergola, Garigliano (with Connecta as a part), Panetteria, She squat, Metropolix, s.q.o.t.t.

During the 90s in Florence (and still today) there existed two large social centers: the CPA in the south and Ex Emerson (now nEXt Emerson) in the north. Both are important for the story told in this book: the CPA as it hosted the first Italian Hackmeeting; Ex-Emerson because Strano Network emerged inside it, a very interesting group in the landscape of early Italian digital activism.

But Florence also hosted many other occupied spaces: Maf, Indiano, Giungla, Baracca, Bubusette, Matticao, Villa, Yoda House, Mulino... For over twenty years the Housing Rights Movement (Movimento di Lotta per la Casa) had led a tough and intensive campaign, combating the fragmentation of working class areas and fighting the crisis of affordable housing through hundreds of occupations involving both Italians and migrants. At the end of the 90s there was also a somewhat exuberant group of students who launched several occupations. One in particular comes up repeatedly during the interviews – the Cecco Rivolta squat.

A fertile environment developed around this space: a weekly paper designed to be pasted on the walls of the city; a campaign for urban gardens; a housing advisory service for students, Omme, which contributed to the proliferation of squats in the city. Between 2000 and 2002 squatted houses popped up like mushrooms: il Pacaro, il Pettirosso, il Bomba libera tutti, il Soqquadro... A substantial community of hundreds of students and casualized workers was created: La Rete (the Network), which took up many issues beyond housing, such as copyright, DIY culture, and the free circulation of knowledge.

These are more or less the environments around which the collective formed. Depending on the city the specifics vary somewhat, but fundamentally the situations were similar.

Before proceeding with our story there is one more element to be put in position. In 1999 in Seattle, thousands of people protested the meeting of the World Trade Organization (WTO). The images were transmitted all over the world and it was as if an imaginary voice had shouted 'Beat It!' Over the following two years each international summit met opposition from tens of thousands. Civil society seemed to rouse itself a little and the Social Forums were born – com-

---

35   *Decoder:* Influential German cyberpunk film directed by Muscha (1984), that gave its name to a
     BBS, a collective, and an eponymous magazine. Established in Milan in 1986, the Decoder collective
     fused elements from punk and squatter culture with the emerging imagination of cyberpunk and
     digital networks. Decoder and those around it were key drivers of the formulation of a computer-based
     communication hypothesis in Italy during that period.

posite assemblies with the ambition of constructing a grassroots alternative to the globalizing processes of big business. However fragile, inexperienced, and inconclusive, one had the sense of being part of an international movement. At every counter-summit demonstrators converged from all over. Davos,[36] Prague,[37] Nice, Naples, and Gothenburg were all stops on this strange 'tour'. In order to reach these destinations, trains and buses were organized – something in between a school trip and an away game.[38] The reality of these demonstrations were far from festive, however…

March 2001, Naples: the demonstration is heavily baton-charged in Piazza Municipio.[39] Those detained are brought to the Raniero barracks[40] and tortured.

June 2001, Gothenburg: the police open fire and injure a young man who remains in a coma for a week. This is a warmup for the G8 in July of the same year, when hundreds of thousands of people take to the streets of Genoa. During three days of demonstrations, Carlo Giuliani is killed by a Carabiniere[41] on Friday. The police baton-charge people indiscriminately until late afternoon. On the Saturday the demonstration is split into several segments, the demonstrators' campsites are raided, and in the evening there is a blitz on the school buildings hosting the media center: the Pascoli and the Diaz/Pertini[42] schools. At the latter those inside are beaten to a bloody pulp and carted off on stretchers. Many of those detained during those days are held in Bolzaneto barracks where they are tortured and abused.

That was our Genoa.

If while reading this you think, 'Yes, the police were out of order, but amongst the demonstrators there were those who threw stones and smashed windows…', then you should consider putting this book down now.

The summer of 2001 is also the moment when the prehistory of A/I comes to an end, because that June the project is officially unveiled at the Hackmeeting in Catania, Sicily. Immediately afterwards almost everyone takes part in the protests against the G8 in Genoa, and any remaining innocence is lost forever: it is clear how the world works. The scenario has changed, the collective exists and has to somehow face the whirlwind.

---

36   Davos: Each year this Swiss mountain resort hosts the World Economic Forum, a gathering of political and corporate bigwigs. As a talking shop of neoliberal capitalism, it has been targeted by protestors since the 1990s.
37   Prague: In September 2000 the International Monetary Fund held a meeting in Prague. This was the first international summit held in Europe since the protests against the World Trade Organization meeting in Seattle the previous year and the anti-summit wave was picking up momentum.
38   The Italian term used here is *trasferta* which refers to collective expeditions made in support of one's team in another city or country.
39   Piazza Municipio: One of the largest squares in Europe and important square in Naples, location also of the city administration.
40   Raniero: Carabinieri barracks in Naples.
41   Carabinieri: Italy has two principal police organizations: the Polizia dello Stato and the Carabinieri. The latter are semi-militarized and live in barracks. Military service can be served in the Carabinieri as an alternative to the army. Carlo Giuliani was killed by one such conscript, Mario Placanica, in Genoa 2001.
42   Pascoli and the Diaz/Pertini schools: These were spaces allocated to the Genoa Social Forum by the City Council.

Hacktivism, 1990-2000

Most of us in the A/I collective come from the generation that grew up with home computing, when the machines became household appliances. During the 1980s the VIC-20, Commodore 64, ZX Spectrum, Amiga, and Atari ST became commonplace.[43] Every member of the collective had one. We were the first generation who grew up with a computer around, mostly as a playmate. As we wore out our joysticks and eyes with video games, data communication took its first steps toward the conquest of the telephone lines thanks to a device invented in the late 1970s: the modem, which made it possible to access the world of home-spun databases and bulletin-board systems (BBSs). BBSs were fundamentally messaging systems, similar to what is now email, combined with a way to exchange files. The most interesting part was how the nodes in these networks communicated, which was very collaborative and captivating. Essentially, you switched on your computer modem late at night, because call charges were lower then, and let people connect to your BBS. Soon BBS networks arose. Some were international like FidoNet, others dedicated to a single topic. They were often deliberately disconnected from the larger network in order to maintain a certain degree of independence and autonomous management, even if they used the same protocols and software. This is why they were called Fido-compatible.

The movement was highly suspicious of technology, especially of computers. This position was not without reason: technology is not neutral. It is developed with specific goals and objectives, which in our money-based world often overlap with a logic of profit that operates above any ethical consideration. There is a strain of thought that sees technology as the keystone for the construction of a lasting totalitarian society. This attitude is exemplified by the group of intellectuals known as the Frankfurt School[44] and by George Orwell's novel *1984*. Communications systems become an unstoppable propaganda machine, as embodied in advertising in our commodity society. This analysis describes a trend which is fairly widespread in our society, but excludes some anomalies that strongly influenced the events recounted in this book.

However, it is possible to compare the history of telecommunications in the 1990s to the history of radio. Initially, radio was a mass medium working under the aegis of state control.

---

43 These models were amongst the first wave of truly home computers which began with the Sinclair ZX 81.

44 The Frankfurt School: The Institute for Social Research was founded in Frankfurt am Main in 1922 and became the center for critical thought in Germany until the exile of its principal protagonists in the 1930s. Amongst its best known participants were Theodor Adorno, Max Horkheimer and Herbert Marcuse, and it was the latter who dedicated significant time and print to the question of technology. Marcuse made a distinction between technics (the material means of communication, transportation, production etc.) and technology, which was a mode of production, a system of social relations, as well as 'a manifestation of prevalent thought and behavior patterns, an instrument for control and domination'.

Guglielmo Marconi,[45] one of its creators, or at least one of the first who rushed to patent the invention, was a convinced fascist who was hired by Pope Pius XI[46] to set up the Vatican's radio station. Forty years later this same tool would become the voice of the 1977 movement.[47]

By the 1970s, radio was widespread and fairly easily accessible. In 1974, a decision by the Italian Court of Cassation, the final Court of Appeal for criminal and civil matters in Italy, ended RAI's state monopoly over national radio and television broadcasting.[48] The ether was free: all you needed was a bit of goodwill, a couple of manuals for amateur radio operators and something to say or to play. In a few years loads of local radio stations were created, many in homes; some smelled a business opportunity and quickly turned into commercial stations, and still others arose within the political movements of the time. Besides the well-known Radio Alice[49] in Bologna, we'd like to mention Radio OndaRossa[50] in Rome, born in 1977, which quickly developed into a politicized radio station close to the movement and hasn't budged since. There was a change in its meaning, not only in its use – a reinvention of the usage of this technological fetish.

The history of telecommunications in the 1990s might be read along fairly similar lines.

Some groups linked to the movement sensed the communications potential of the BBS and home computing and its relative independence. Some expressly political BBSs took shape. Some examples include: ZERO! BBS[51] in Turin, which was hosted for a while on Radio Black Out's[52] premises, and all those BBSs which became part of the European Counter Network (ECN) project and are extensively described in the first chapter of this book. ECN aimed at becoming a network of what we might call, for the sake of brevity and fully aware of the poverty

---

45   Guglielmo Marconi: Italian inventor credited with the breakthroughs enabling long distance radio transmission, and founder of the famed Marconi company which commercialized the technology. Marconi joined the Fascist Party in 1923 and became an outspoken defender of its ideology and deeds later in his life.
46   Pius XI: Pope from 1922 to 1939, signatory of the Lateran Treaties between the Catholic Church and Mussolini. This agreement put an end to the unresolved tension born of Italian unification and established the Vatican as a sovereign state.
47   1977 movement: This year was an inflection point in the composition of the movement. Lotta Continua had dissolved in 1976 and other formal organizations failed to develop traction. Instead there appeared a broad politicized youth culture mixing politics with music, sexual emancipation, and direct action. In parallel to this the level of violence was growing and the atmosphere was increasingly militarized. Guido Chiesa's *Lavorare Con Lentezza* provides a portrait of that moment, albeit in a city, Bologna, where the student element predominated over the proletarian.
48   RAI, Radio Televisione Italiana: The Italian public broadcaster, now operating radio, television, and online services, was rebranded as RAI in 1954 having existed under other forms and acronyms since 1924.
49   Radio Alice: Independent radio station set up in Bologna in 1976 by creative activists in and around the autonomist movement. The station was shut down live on air during the riots following the killing of medical student Francesco Lorusso by police in 1977. In 2004 Radio Alice was the subject of a feature film, *Lavorare con Lentezza*, directed by Guido Chiesa.
50   Radio OndaRossa: Long-running movement political station based in the San Lorenzo district of Rome.
51   ZERO! BBS: Bulletin board created in Turin in 1989 by elements of ECN; also part of CyberNet.
52   Radio Black Out: Independent political radio station broadcasting in the Turin area, financially supported by the city's squatted spaces.

of the term, European antagonism.[53] In fact, the BBS system connected to this network existed almost exclusively in Italy. The first nodes were in Rome, Padua, and Florence. Meanwhile another circuit linked to the digital underground scene was emerging – the Cybernet network – which attracted participants more focused on literature, artistic expression, and what we might call the cyberpunk imagination. Among them were Decoder BBS, Virtual Town in Florence, AvANa BBS in Rome, and ECN Bologna, but the nodes would soon number over fifty. In Sicily, Freaknet was formed, a network similar to each of those previously mentioned but independent of both. People in this milieu began talking about hacking, that particular approach to technology and reality that led many members of the A/I collective to meet in person.

In those years there was a small handbook in circulation. In a few lines, it captured some of the ideas we grew up with. It was called *Digital Guerrilla*, and in the chapter 'Movement Networks' it read:

> So what does all this mean to us? One of the main goals of the movement (and for many of us, one of the main goals of our existence) is communication. The communication of ideas in the search for political change, communication among groups to share projects and help in organizing, communication among individuals to form groups (or just to keep their individuality, despite groups), and communication as a means to meet other people in the world with the same interests and goals. Data networks can be a cheap and easy-to-use alternative medium both for inter-personal and mass communication [...] In any case, it would be nice to open up access to the movement's networks to those who don't own a computer. This can be achieved by setting up public terminals in social centers, infoshops,[54] book stores, etc. And possibly also by printing part of the material and distributing it on paper. Through data networks, we can automate the spreading of news and information across the city, the nation and the world: networks don't care about political borders [...] But data networks can become much more than that. Many people, even some of those who already use them, insist on seeing networks merely as a big megaphone for their more or less alternative and counter-cultural initiatives. Actually, such tools are not only great counter-information agencies for traditional militant collectives, they can also give rise to novel community forms. When physical closeness no longer determines the range of our possible experiences, also "educational institutions" like families, relatives or parishes (be they religious or "political") can be seriously weakened [...].[55]

---

53 European antagonism: This phrase is something of a misnomer; 'antagonism' is a rubric that encompasses the various tendencies of left radical politics uninterested in mainstream political lobbying. Anti-institutional and direct action-oriented, as a term it is specific to Italy. There it also designates a period, mainly the 1980s after the decline of the '77 movement, which was decimated by virtual internment and exile following the round-ups of April 1979, where several thousand people were arrested. Some of what survived came to reconstitute itself publicly with a focus on 'opposing imperialism' and involvement in the anti-nuclear campaigns.

54 Infoshops: A hybrid combination of elements of a bookshop, archive, and meeting space. As the name suggests, their focus is on disseminating information. Whilst predominantly a northern European phenomenon, there were some also in Italy during the 1990s.

55 ZERO! and BITs Against The Empire Labs (eds) *Digital Guerrilla. Guida all'uso alternativo di computer, modem e reti telematiche*, 1995, www.ecn.org/zero/digguer.htm. Quote translated by author.

To understand this vision of data networks, it may be worth recalling that FidoNet creator Tom Jennings is a self-defined 'punk, anarchist, libertarian, homosexual, hacker and a promoter of the piracy of any kind of commercial software'.[56] This was a great starting point for us. Meanwhile the internet boomed, the web was created, and BBSs were literally switched off: crushed in part by the Italian Crackdown of 1994,[57] the first annoying and grotesquely repressive encounter between the Italian authorities and ICT. ECN thus was transformed into a server run by the Isole nella Rete collective.[58] Many movement groups hosted their web pages there and held discussions on mailing lists or chat. Cybernet got scattered, its traces left on the #cybernet channel on ircnet and in the cybernet.cyberpunk newsgroup on A/I's news servers.

The community that was born on BBSs only to later migrate to the internet then floated the idea of a meeting. Three days of something midway between workshops, discussions, and a party: the Hackmeeting. As it had been proposed by the scene around the Strano Network project, it took place in Florence in June 1998 in one of the historical social centers of the city – the CPA. Nearly every Italian group was there, meeting face to face for the first time, gathered in the same venue. Listing the participants or describing the atmosphere in detail would be rather useful to frame that period, but would require dozens of pages. We will limit ourselves to noting the presentation of a book whose introduction remains one of the clearest texts to grasp much of the vision from which A/I originated. The book was Kriptonite, a handbook on how to use cryptography and avoid the control implicit in a computerized society. Aside from any judgment on this analysis, that introduction is a perfect synthesis of the spirit of those years.

After that first test, the Hackmeeting became an annual appointment organized via a mailing list, and it came to be a fertile soil in which at least part of A/I matured. The Hackmeetings that followed took place in Milan, then in Rome, and in 2001 in Catania, Sicily. Catania was the occasion when A/I was officially unveiled, but it was during the Milan Hackmeeting that the LOA group – frequently mentioned in the interviews – came into being. What was articulated in particular was the need to set up local structures midway between clubs and laboratories that would work as year-round connective tissue for the Hackmeeting community. These hacklabs soon started to appear, often located in social centers, combining elements of the workshop and experimentation. Hacklab activity focused frequently on education, such as courses and the sharing of knowledge, and on the ability to use or at least understand digital tools.

---

56 Helena Velena, talk at *Diritto alla comunicazione nello scenario di fine millennio – Iniziativa nazionale in difesa della telematica amatoriale*, Conference by Strano Network, Centro per l'Arte Contemporanea Luigi Pecci, 19 February 1995, Prato, http://www.strano.net/snhtml/atticonv/velena.htm.

57 The Italian Crackdown of 1994: This refers to the first major series of raids against Italian BBSs, launched at the behest of prosecutors in Pesaro, Turin, and Taranto. This investigation resulted in the seizure of dozens of computers and other equipment on the pretext that it was being used for software piracy. This episode catalyzed the creation of organizations such as the *Associazione per la libertà nella comunicazione elettronica interattiva* (ALCEI), with the purpose of defending civil rights in the new digital public sphere. The phrase 'Italian crackdown' intentionally echoes the phraseology used by Bruce Sterling in his classic account of the police raids against hackers which triggered the creation of the EFF in the United States in 1990, the *Hacker Crackdown*.

58 Isole nella Rete collective: 'Islands in the Net' was the name of the collective formed to operate ECN's server for movement-related material and websites. It was born as the web exploded and the BBS culture declined. The name was inspired by a cyberpunk novel written by Bruce Sterling and published in 1988.

Two events within the ICT world created the technological basis for a huge number of projects, as well as the educational basis for most hacklabs: in 1991 the first version of Linux was released. Even before that a weird guy called Richard Stallman[59] started the GNU project and came up with the term 'free software' to define a particular way of developing and sharing programs – they should be released together with their source code and all code derived from them would in turn have to follow some simple rules. These two events created the technological basis for a huge number of projects, as well as the educational basis for most hacklabs. For example, A/I's servers use Debian/GNU Linux, one of the oldest Linux distributions.

Meanwhile in the rest of the world the new economy was booming: companies were off-shoring production, the internet's existence was being noticed, and there was a headfirst charge towards the gold rush of the dot-com domains. The market went nuts and the Nasdaq[60] fibrillated in excitement like a teenager during his first sexual experience. And like an unskilled and hasty lover, it came too soon. In 2000 the new economy reached a peak and then stagnated: the dot-com bubble burst, and many firms that had staked everything on offering web services went bust. But in just a few years the cokehead craze of the markets had changed the face of the web.

It's not by chance that during this period a protest tactic was born that is still used today: the netstrike. This means to overwhelm a website by simultaneously connecting to it from too many thousands of computers. From 1995 onwards netstrikes were launched in support of every kind of campaign: from Chiapas[61] to protests against the eviction of the CPA in Florence or the Bulk in Milan, to the G8 in Genoa. It began years before many Italian institutions and large businesses had any online presence at all, even an email address.

---

59   Richard Stallman: Charismatic founder of the GNU ('GNU's Not Unix') project in 1983 whose aim was to develop a fully functional operating system which would enshrine four fundamental user freedoms in its licensing provisions. Exercising these freedoms requires access to the source code of the program so that the user can: run the program for any purpose, study the code, modify it, and/or redistribute it in original or improved form. Software produced on such terms is referred to as free software. GNU/Linux is the most famous and fundamental free software project as it constitutes a full operating system which enables users to exit the world of Apple iOS and Windows. GNU/Linux is distributed in many different flavors, the best-known being Ubuntu, whose development is managed by the Canonical corporation. Debian on the other hand is the biggest community-based GNU/Linux distribution, assembled and monitored by almost one thousand volunteer 'maintainers'.

60   Nasdaq: The world's first electronic stock market, established in 1971. Since the first dotcom boom it has been the preferred location for technology companies to publicly float, i.e. offer shares to the general public.

61   Chiapas: The southernmost region of Mexico and home of the Zapatista rebel movement which launched an insurgency against neoliberalism on the 1 January 1995, the same day as the North American Free Trade Agreement came into effect. In 1996 Subcommandant Marcos, spokesperson for the Zapatistas, made a call for an independent communication network, a call he was to repeat to a gathering of alternative media activists. '[…] In August 1996, we called for the creation of a network of independent media, a network of information. We mean a network to resist the power of the lie that sells us this war that we call the Fourth World War. We need this network not only as a tool for our social movements, but for our lives: this is a project of life, of humanity, humanity which has a right to critical and truthful information'. Subcomandante Marcos, 'Statement of Subcomandante Marcos to the Freeing the Media Teach-In', *Tactical Media* Crew, 31 January/1 February 1997, https://www.tmcrew. org/chiapas/e_media1.htm.

The availability of these means of communication, the political reflection on how to use them, and the need to talk about the growing movement gave rise to a new body in the Italian landscape. In the year 2000, Indymedia Italy was born, an experiment in open publishing, managed through a number of mailing lists. A large community joined this project: video makers, nerds, aspiring journalists, and more traditional activists. Indymedia quickly became a reference point on the web for the whole movement, which, for better or worse, populated the newswires with articles and comments. During the G8 in Genoa it turned out to be some-what instrumental, thanks to its ability to narrate what was happening in real time and give an unfiltered voice to the movement, with all its multiple and contradictory spirits. And here we return once again to Genoa in 2001, and a July choking on tear gas.

The ECN Experience

In 1988, the Danish group TV Stop[62] proposed the launch of a shared European data com-munications network for the antagonist movement. The European Counter-Information Net-work, or ECN, was a plan to create many national networks connected at the supranational level. In Italy, the project was run by what was then called the National Anti-imperialist and Anti-nuclear Network, or the 'Anti-Anti'.

Snd: *The Italians who attended TV Stop's meeting were Radio Sherwood[63] from Padua, Zom-bi_J from Bologna and Radio OndaRossa from Rome. On their return, they began to reflect on the political meaning of the emergence of these new technologies. What it was all about was setting up a BBS network that linked together alternative political projects, the groups of the radical left that were scattered all over Europe and that at the time, 1988-1989, were still extremely sparse, very linked to local issues and to current events. In Padua, they set up a BBS node with amateur FidoNet technology borrowed from the Americans – you could connect by using a telephone, a modem and a computer.*

In 1989 the first experimental connections took place, and in 1990 ECN was born, divided among the Italian nodes of Padua, Florence, and Rome. Bologna and Turin followed and eventually Milan too had a node.

Snd: *We liked the idea from the start, but in Milan it didn't catch on straight away. At Leon-cavallo there was great resistance – in those years the computer was something you'd find at work, the firm would put it there to make you work more, it was a tool of the capitalists. The IT communication collective was already born, and half a dozen people joined the original four members. We offered courses on how to use a computer with the aim of being legitimated as a group. After a lot of effort and lending a hand at the bar, we somehow managed to buy a computer and get the Milanese node online in 1991.*

---

62   TV Stop: Danish TV station operated by squatters from 1987 to 2012 in Christiania, later operating out of a studio in Nørrebro, also in Copenhagen. Documentation available in Danish at *tvstop.dk*. The station no longer exists in its original form and is now operated by Kurdish groups.

63   Radio Sherwood: Independent radio station broadcasting out of Padua in the Veneto region of Italy. This station is closely associated with a regionally embedded left radical tradition which stretches from Potere Operaio (1967-73) in the 1970s to the Disobbedienti/White Overalls at the turn of the century. Today they operate www.globalproject.info.

There were already a dozen nodes when the project was officially presented at the International Meeting in Venice[64] in June 1991, where around two thousand Italians and internationals met to discuss new forms of social conflict. The meeting began with a reflection on how to extend the network to the rest of Europe, but in fact Italy was the only national territory to implement the proposal that emanated from TV Stop. But the idea started to spread, and in the Netherlands XS4ALL launched an initiative to provide internet access for all, which started from the alternative cultural sphere but was dressed up as a commercial provider. In Germany, the Autonomen movement[65] gave birth to SpinnenNetz (Spidernet), a network formed by groups on the radical left.

Snd: *Between the late 1980s and the early 1990s a world of communication emerged that was completely new compared to the classical forms – newspapers, magazines or television. In the States there was Usenet, and the internet was a tool usable for everyone, even if the technology was only accessible to a small elite.*

Two different modes of understanding the potential of amateur telecommunications emerged from the first nationwide workshops and meetings that were organized to discuss the ECN network. On the one hand there was ECN, the titular collective that maintained the ECN network and saw it as a means of political action; on the other hand, there was a more diverse milieu, including elements of Decoder, AvANa BBS from Rome,[66] and la Cayenna from Feltre, who viewed it as a 'new frontier of human action, based on a new, rhizomatic mode of communication'.[67]

Snd: *At the time there were already more evolved analyses, like those by Decoder, who were somehow our 'family-enemies'. We had two opposed visions. For years they had been promoting a cultural vision that focused on hacking and the changes that the new technology would bring about in the world and society: a very lofty vision. On the other hand, our idea was functionalist, utilitarian: we needed a tool to create links among the participants of the movement, the collectives, the social centers, and individual activists.*

For the Milanese part of the ECN collective, the political context could not be set aside, especially as this was the period between 1989 and 1992 when the so-called 'social centers movement' arose. In Milan such ferment had not been seen for a decade.

Snd: *In the wake of the eviction and reoccupation of Leoncavallo on the 16 August 1989, a series of small and large occupations began. They were suddenly in the limelight, and tried to get exposure and set a political agenda, even at the micro level of the alternative world. A further meaningful aspect of those years was the Panther student movement, whose main characteristic was their co-ordination through fax machines – in fact, it was also known as 'the*

---

64   International Meeting in Venice: This meeting of the radical left included a series of parallel thematic tracks, one of which was media & communications. Participants included ECN, Decoder, The Chaos Computer Club from Hamburg, Germany, and the Austrian group Zerberus.

65   Autonomen: German left radical movement. Orthographic similarity to 'autonomi' and 'autonomia' notwithstanding, this movement has its own distinct character, wedding the heritage of communist organizations from the 1970s with elements of alternative culture.

66   AvANa BBS: Avana BBS was based in Rome and later became a Hacklab inside the squatted Napoleonic Fort, Forte Prenestino.

67   A. Di Corinto, T. Tozzi, coauthors of *Hacktivism: La libertà nelle maglie della rete*, Roma: Manifestolibri, 2002, www.hackerart.org/storia/hacktivism.htm.

fax movement'. From the occupied administration offices of the universities, students would send tons of faxes as did social centers, to spread the news of new occupations, picket lines, etc. These were the premises of something that was getting bigger, that was evolving. People believed that a movement was being born or reborn, we saw new faces, and what arose within this flowering was also the idea that we could use different tools, like the Panther movement's fax. In this context, we also began to think that computers could be tools for creating links, for exchanging information, for sharing things.

During the early 1990s, ECN's objectives gradually changed, going beyond what had been the aims of the 'Anti-Anti' organization – they tried to reach out to every group in the movement that was not using digital tools, by converting their documents into a digital format, as well as putting them in touch with each other.

Snd: *Every Saturday and Sunday we would go to places with groups of people who wanted to create their own node, which almost never happened because there was an insurmountable technological barrier. To set up a node, a huge amount of skill was required. In the end, very few were created: in our heyday, there were nine boxes plus three or four 'user nodes' (points), which could connect to the BBS system natively once in a while to download new messages. This way, however, we managed to disseminate the communications of the social centers. We were few – myself and a couple of others at Leoncavallo, someone in Rome from via dei Volsci[68] – at Radio OndaRossa – someone at Radio Sherwood. We received tons of faxes, typed them into a computer and disseminated them via the net. We felt that it had great potential, so much so that in 1993-1995 we tried to give birth to a parallel experience, a sort of AP of the radical left and a service for the movement's radio stations.*

Having such an extraordinary and diverse range of interests, the 'data communications move-ment' was growing alongside but independent of the initiatives of individual social centers. In Milan, ECN published fanzines and magazines with news that only circulated in online networks, they put out a weekly bulletin and much more.

Snd: *Just think of ECN's bulletin; two hundred copies were printed on Monday evening… Nobody had seen anything similar since Lotta Continua's magazine.[69] At the time some said that it wasn't an unfair comparison. We measured ourselves against them…*

By the mid-1990s, the 'Anti-Anti' organization had dissolved, relationships among social centers had started to change and there were several splits. The movement as it was known went into crisis. As a consequence, ECN began to be underused and attracted less interest than before. At the same time different approaches to the web began to emerge.

Snd: *There were some 'good-for-nothings' who immediately thought about other uses for these tools… The Luther Blissett collective was born… In Bologna some people started to use ECN for a very deep critique of the social centers. Some considered themselves the heirs*

---

68   Via dei Volsci: Street in Rome's San Lorenzo district well known as a hotbed of extra-parliamentary activity and HQ to the city's wing of Autonomia Operaia who published a magazine titled *i Volsci*.

69   Lotta Continua: Born in 1969, LC was the biggest organization of the heterodox far left with a strong orientation towards grassroots movements. As the 70s progressed it began to run candidates in elections and faced increasing internal tensions especially over gender questions, culminating in its dissolution in 1976. LC published a daily newspaper which continued to be printed until 1982.

of Autonomia Operaia,[70] but Autonomia Operaia was dead and buried, and even the social context had changed. It was a nostalgic idea, just like a number of principles that passed from the radical left wing to the small world of the social centers, which was actually totally different... If Lenin had seen something like that, he would have shot them immediately, he would have sent them to Siberia without thinking twice! We had punk concerts on Saturday nights, in a social center the economy was based on the bar, where hundreds of gallons of beer were sold every night and weed was everywhere... The idea of being heirs to anything was baseless. In social centers there were older political groups and there were younger people who said: 'everything's different now'. There was a split in ECN too, with those who weren't comfortable with this change and the idea that tools could be used in a different way, to start a dialogue that went beyond how things were traditionally discussed and addressed society as it was.

Meanwhile, at a meeting in Florence in January 1993, some people decided to create an independent network with gateways open to any network that requested it. The CyberNet was thus born. The first connection was established with the node of Senza Confine BBS in Macerata, which acted as a national hub for all communications, and with Hacker Art BBS in Florence. In March and April Decoder BBS from Milan and Bits Against the Empire from Trento connected to the network.

Snd: *ECN's network had declined and contracted. In order to keep it functioning, we Milanese got in touch with other FidoNet networks, like P-net, which re-established a connection between us and Decoder's network.*

Unlike ECN's network, CyberNet is a rhizomatic network, i.e. it is based on a horizontal model with message areas where everybody can read and write. CyberNet's main message area was Cyberpunk, a common area originally shared by ECN and P-net and subsequently also by Freaknet and other networks. In its first year CyberNet reached twenty something nodes, nearly fifty in its second.

Snd: *In 1993-1994 the web was invented at CERN. Jerry Cornelius,[71] who worked in IT and was interested in innovation, showed me one of the first screens and told me: 'Look, this is the future'. So we got interested in this new thing.*

The advent of the internet actually opened a new season for ECN-Milan. In 1995, Isole nella Rete (Islands in the Net) was founded together with a website that contained all of ECN's contents as well as its main message areas, now turned into mailing lists. The first lists were: *Movimento* (Movement), on the political activities of alternative Italian movements; *CS-List*, on the activities of social centers; *Internazionale* (International), on international news; and

---

70   The name here does not refer to an organization in a traditional sense but rather a confluence of groups sharing similar characteristics. This quality is captured in Italian by the phrase 'Area dell'Autonomia', - the area of autonomy. The component elements emanated from workplace committees in large factories, student and neighborhood collectives, and subversive cultural groups involved in independent radio stations and publications such as A/Traverso. Low-level political violence was common during this period and as the ante rose the groups around the autonomia were pinched between state repression on the one side and organized armed groups like the Red Brigades on the other. Some plunged into the armed struggle themselves, some walked away and others were targeted in the mass police round-ups in 1979.

71   Nickname inspired by a character from Michael Moorcock's books.

ECN news, ECN's newsletter. Later other lists were created: *EZLN It*, supporting the Zapatista rebellion in Chiapas; cyber-rights, on freedom of communication as a right; *Antipro*, on anti-prohibitionist topics; and *Deviazioni* (Deviations), on homosexual issues. After these, the new platform opened the first websites managed by Italian antagonist groups, like Tactical Media Crew and Malcolm X from Rome or Strano Network from Florence.

Snd: *With the internet a new horizon opened. Jerry and I started to think about this and suggested a meeting with members of the other collectives that had strayed from the path. In August 1995, at Radio Onda d'Urto's party in Brescia, a dozen of us had a meeting and we proposed making the jump to the internet. In the wake of TV Stop's proposal meanwhile, Radio Sherwood from Padua had set up a server with XS4ALL, a Dutch commercial server basically created by some comrades. People in Bologna and Rome had found a space that could host their few web pages too, whereas we wanted to create a server of our own. They answered that it didn't make sense to centralize in a moment when the web was expanding, but we did it anyway because we thought it was a good idea. As a group, ECN-Milan organized events in social centers as part of an ECN-tour: we demonstrated the internet and explained that it could be more than a simple technological change, that it could offer other opportunities for communication. By involving people who had participated in the projects in other cities over the years, we found the resources to buy a computer and sign a contract with a provider. In March 1996 we founded the association Isole nella Rete and everything began. On the 1 August we went online, and while many had still some doubts, we Milanese believed in what we were doing.*

ECN became the first virtual network of the Italian movement, the first group offering mailboxes, websites, and, above all, indispensable mailing lists. With time, the web was considered not only a structure for distribution, but also a political subject in itself. Not without difficulties, Isole nella Rete managed to maintain an autonomous position, asserting itself as a tool for everybody rather than the property of a particular social center. The aim was to offer opportunities for communication and building relations in a world marked by dynamics of fragmentation and political confrontation.

Snd: *It worked, and even those who had put their pages up somewhere else, moved them to ECN's server. By building a space that anybody could access, we gained great visibility in a moment when the means of communication were fragmented. This was actually one of the elements that helped our initiative succeed. People knew that if they accessed ecn.org, they would find information and publications from Italy's alternative left wing – social centers, free radios, collectives, etc. It was there, it was visible. And this goal was pretty difficult to reach.*

In 1998 ECN-Isole nella Rete offered the first anonymous remailer in Italy – an important instrument for protecting people's privacy and fostering communication among activists. That experience and the materials created for it would become Kriptonite, a book published the same year, leaving a vital legacy to the new generations just entering the digital world.

Snd: *Our experience as ECN finished in the mid-1990s, whereas Isole nella Rete's end came in the second half of the decade. Other projects followed, as they would have anyway. I'm thinking about Indymedia, which had independent origins and did extremely interesting things, probably more than we did, or about the experience of Inventati, Autistici, and that whole bunch of messers – or young punks, as I called them.*

In our story, the year 1998 was a turning point. In 1998, so to speak, an era finished and a new one began. This shift happened with the organization of the first Hackmeeting, which would then become the annual meeting of digital countercultures.

Snd: *1998 saw the first interesting activity that went beyond the tradition of the former collectives. In Florence they brought the first Hackmeeting to life. In the beginning, the collective that managed Isole nella Rete was a bit doubtful about this proposal, because it wasn't very political. Then we all went and liked it so much that the next year we did it in Milan.*

That was the turning point that brought the ECN collective out of Leoncavallo, and in some way, also marked the end of that experience. In Milan, in 1999, the ECN-Milan collective split up and LOA was born in the Bulk. It was a new era: the era of hacker laboratories.

The Greater Milan Area – Autistici

At the final assembly of the 1998 Hackmeeting at the CPA in Florence, it was decided to hold another the following year in Milan. ECN and Decoder,[72] the two groups active on the digital front in the Lombard capital, were given responsibility for its organization and opened a dedicated discussion list: Hackit99.

Blicero: *Decoder was fundamental to our education, inspiration, and imagination, and it was their network of relationships that made it possible to put together the Hackmeeting. I always had an excellent rapport with Decoder because it was through reading their magazine that I realized the centrality of technological issues. Unfortunately during the organization of the '99 Hackmeeting there was a fight between the politically active milieu from ECN, and the more countercultural, technological, and philosophical crowd of Decoder. Following the row, Decoder stepped back from the Hackmeeting.*

In 1998, Blicero was part of Bredaoccupata 3337, a space that he described as innovative and characterized by radical political choices. Based on his own enthusiasm and an intuition that communications and technology are strategic political arenas, he proposed to organize evenings on these subjects and took responsibility for getting in touch with ECN.

Blicero: *I first heard of ECN at Sintesi (another squat) but we only met when I contacted them to arrange an event at Breda, what would later become Neuromacchine. In Milan there was a good synergy with the old nucleus of ECN from the outset. I proposed that we meet and start work on the next Hackmeeting.*

To launch Hackmeeting '99 a range of actions were organized including a warmup. Five nights in different Milanese social centers – Leoncavallo, Cox18, S.q.o.t.t., Deposito Bulk and of course, Breda, with Neuromacchine. Meanwhile the Bulk depot – recently squatted by students – was prepared for the event and hosted the Hackmeeting between the 18 and 20 June 1999.

Bomboclat: *At the closing assembly of Hackmeeting '99, the campaign to open hacklabs throughout Italy was launched. Meanwhile in Milan, ECN – who had moved from Leoncavallo*

---

72   In this case, the collective and namesake magazine established in Milan in 1986.

to the Bulk – opened LOA with the younger hackers. Once the project can stand on its own two feet, Snd, Graziano, and the other oldtimers step aside so as to avoid unduly influencing the youngsters.

With the group that had organized and catalyzed the Hackmeeting, LOA in Milan was born. The new hacklab borrowed its name from William Gibson's cyberpunk universe where *loas* are curious voodoo spirits, cultural archetypes incarnated in the structures of the network and technology, forces of the collective unconscious.

Pbm: *I didn't read science fiction, nor was I interested in cyberpunk but I was into digital rights…*

The Hackmeeting turned out to be a crucial meeting point, because it brought into contact people who came from very different backgrounds but shared the same attitude towards computing.

Shah: *Everything started with the coordination list, but we knew each other only as digital beings, as avatars on the list. I got in touch electronically with the group organizing the Hackmeeting, but it was only during the organization phase and the preliminary events that I began to meet them in person. Immediately there was a familiarity. After the success of Hackit99, we said 'Ok, when shall we meet again?!'*

The new group occupied a room in the Bulk, a natural continuation after hosting the Hackmeeting. They started to meet on a regular basis, originally coordinated through what had been the Hackit99 list, which, having closed the archives, became theirs. Part of the original Milanese collective of Isole nella Rete also merged with LOA, giving the new project many 'founding fathers'.

Shah: *The first years were pure cultural enrichment, not only in terms of hacking but also in terms of relationships. Wildly disparate people, coming from very different contexts and situations, were able to share their knowledge. At the beginning we did it in a completely informal way between ourselves; somebody who knew something explained it to the others… together we learned how to rebuild computers from different pieces of hardware, to make them work and get them online… and what we just knew ourselves was already an amazing source of information.*

At LOA hardware was recycled and a torrent of activities tied to the hacker imagination took place. Sitting down in front of a computer and deciding what to do, everyone followed their own inclinations and learned through experimentation.

Blicero: *In reality not a lot was done that first year, seminars were organized, and there were discussions of technology as liberation… Let's call it a constructive moment from an existential perspective.*

On New Year's Eve 2000, while the Bulk was under threat of eviction, LOA took part in the squatting of an old ENEL warehouse. The new venue became operational after the eviction from the property at via Don Sturzo on the 2 March. In the new Bulk, in via Niccolini, the LOA-Hacklab grabbed a nice slice of space: two rooms in the turret.

Blicero: *One could say that was when LOA was truly born. Until then it was a space within a space; it didn't subscribe to the politics of the Bulk but contributed in its own way. Now that we had squatted it, the space felt more like ours. The turret of the new Bulk was truly our ivory tower.*

The same year another group using the Bulk asked LOA to give a course on HTML. They were the authors of the e-zine Chainworkers and their goal was to enable all of their editors to directly participate in their online publishing.

Bomboclat: *Zoe and her friend Laura organized a truly unforgettable course, I don't know how many writers for Chainworkers took part, but it was a tremendous inspiration for us to push ahead and offer more classes.*

Once it was understood that their accumulated knowledge was also useful to the other inhabitants of planet Earth, the playful instinct gave way to an educational urge and new computer courses were organized for the community.

Pbm: *To do the courses we needed a classroom, teaching materials, computers, and structure. Those who knew how to set up networks, set up the networks. Those who knew how to repair the benches, repaired the benches.*

During this training LOA developed a series of increasingly daring ideas, that emulated or anticipated what was happening in other Italian cities. Lessons were organized in reverse engineering, UNIX, programming in C, and in a moment of enthusiasm, even a Chinese class.

Bomboclat: *Our motto was: 'technical problems don't exist'. Somebody always turned out be the key to solving any particular problem. Every type of skill set converged in LOA. In addition to the technician who salvaged the hardware, there were experts in one thing or another, programmers, system administrators…*

Historically, LOA was one of the first modern hacklabs, born after those in Florence and Rome – which had already existed as BBS nodes – and the Freaknet Medialab in Catania.

Caparossa: *Apart from AvANA BBS in Rome and Freaknet – which already existed – the Florence hacklab was the first in the wave. For two or three years after the '99 meeting, hacklabs were born everywhere even in the unlikeliest of places like Asti.[73]*

With the transition to the internet, self-managed computer labs emerged everywhere and it was there that an entire generation learned about new technologies. Thanks to the hacklabs, Hackmeetings, and servers like kyuzz.org and tmcrew.org[74] (which like ECN offered services to the Italian digital community), the exchanges intensified between different contexts and experiences, but were united by a common world view.

Psykozygo: *An idea launched on a list was discussed in IRC, bounced to a newsgroup, changed form and became enriched, then became something concrete in a way that was never originally imagined.*

---

73   Asti: Small city of 75,000 people located in northwestern Italy, not far from Turin.
74   tmcrew.org: The server of Tactical Media Crew, a media collective active in Rome from 1995 until the early 2000s.

It was in this period of explosive communication that the motto '+kaos' took shape. Since then, it has been bound in some way to the history of A/I.

Alieno: *A couple of times I tried to reconstruct the first occasion* +kaos *appeared online, but each time there's a different version. Somehow the term* +kaos *is literally a loa, a tiny spirit from the Italian net from the early 00s.*

Although from the start, these places by their very nature taught people how to use a computer, understanding it at both hardware and software levels, LOA soon started providing systematic training. Within a few months, there were two computer courses a day, attended by a lot of people with many different interests.

Bomboclat: *For years these seminars offered better training than the schools.*

But the Milanese hacklab wasn't only a place chosen by chance where people understood that knowledge is power and should be shared. For the guys who met there, LOA quickly became a hyperspace where each individual's curiosities and interests met, melded and fit perfectly; this went on to define a shared existential journey.

Pbm: *In LOA suddenly everything fit. No longer did I have separate musical, digital and ideological spheres. So I basically lived there for a year – so many things and projects were born.*

The hackers of LOA wanted their practices to reflect the anarchistic nature of the internet. They worked hard at this, in order to escape the logic that they saw in other groups, dynamics that seem to inevitably lead to hierarchical relationships, and slowly to the suppression of the possibility of inventing yourself every day. Not only did they do these things together, they also attempted to teach themselves how to manage relationships and share power.

Pbm: *I saw real change in the way people interacted with one another. Personally my ideas were immature and confused, developed alone, but I started making sense of them by being with people coming from a milieu with a strong political consciousness that I lacked. LOA was a place for encounters and communication, not just for the sharing of technical knowledge.*

Because of their tendency to communicate in what one might describe as an unorthodox manner, they decided to call themselves 'The Autistics'. To the rest of the world ten people in a room communicating via chat instead of face to face could seem like a scene of complete estrangement, a metaphor for the new alienation.

Pbm: *One of the motives for autisticization came from the fact that one works alone at a computer. The computer has only one monitor and only one keyboard and is closed off because contact with others isn't necessary. But a computer can be used differently. In LOA I learned this (along with so many other things, both from a technical and interpersonal point of view).*

Maybe LOA became a unique group by sharing this new, unusual modality of being together to overcome the isolating exterior of computers; by so doing they learned a different way to make decisions, one that goes in the other direction.

Pbm: *But we realized that our communication skills and our openness remained limited. We became aware of it, for example, communicating with other collectives inside the Bulk. Every* *single day the contrast was front and center. From that we realized that if we wanted to do something that would truly put our skills to use, we needed to integrate with others who were more communicative, dedicated to invention.*

Florence – Inventati

Meanwhile, Inventati was born in Florence, only it was known then as *Sgamati*.

Cojote: *Before Inventati, Sgamati was the reference point. Since we'd decided that we needed to work on news online, we got this thing together. There was me, Anoushow, Ilnonsubire, and Mille, but there were other people around. We didn't have great technical skills but thanks to people from the hacklab – Ferry Byte, TheWalrus, and others who had been part of ECN – we started some websites. From the beginning our idea was to cover protests and other movement activities. Really we were a small group improvising in a pre-Indymedia period.*

At the core of Inventati was a group of people connected to the student collectives, barely out of their teens.

Pinke: *I didn't join Sgamati immediately, but we were part of the same scene. Sgamati was born as an informal project with a series of people orbiting around it – only later did it become stable. We were all friends and a few were part of Sgamati while a couple did other stuff… but at night it was always the same crowd drinking beer together…*

It was late 1998, early 1999. A lot was going on politically and like their peers, they were active in the Autonomist Movement[75] without directly joining any of the established local groups. Brutal experiences were not long in coming, and during the general strike against the war in Kosovo[76] they had their first encounter with state repression.

Pinke: *On the 13 May 1999 there was a short march that finished with a brutal attack by the police in front of the American Consulate. Defenseless people were chased and beaten; it's our first experience of police violence. Anoushow ended up in hospital. From then on, we understood that for passionate youngsters, protest could involve taking a beating or getting arrested. Afterwards, the newspapers wrote stuff about 'the Autonomists' guerrilla warfare' – they stigmatized and blamed us. We thought about it and concluded that if things turn that way in the streets, we'd have to report it ourselves, because journalists will only write bullshit.*

This traumatic experience reinforced the insight that audio and video produced during a demo can be useful, and they began to show up in the streets with video cameras. For the first time it was participants – and not just journalists or police – carrying this equipment and they had to fight with organizers, 'old timers' who instinctively distrusted it.

---

75 Autonomist movement: In the original text the reference is once again to 'antagonismo'. Antagonism is a broad term embracing many different ideological groups and used to fudge the differences between them. It resembles the use later made of 'autonomi', autonomists, after this term had broken away from its original reference to Autonomia Operaia. The picture is further complicated by the fact that many collectives directly integrated the word antagonismo into their names. these groups often strove to maintain the legacy of the movement of the 70s through the difficult decade that followed.

76 The war in Kosovo began in February 1998 and continued until June the following year. From March to June 1999 NATO carried out a large scale air campaign using air bases in Italy.

Pbm: *For the long-standing militants, technology meant the tools of social control. It took time to win the movement's trust.*

After some initial discussion, their gadgets were accepted. In part because they were always at demonstrations and therefore rather unlikely infiltrators, but also because the presence of a camera within the march sometimes played out in the movement's favor. That was how the movement came to recognize its value as a tool of struggle.

Cojote: *The crucial episode happened during a protest by the Housing Rights Movement in via Cavour. A policeman rang the doorbell to an apartment on the street, introduced himself as a journalist, and asked to come up to take photos from the balcony. Several politically active students were living there and they became suspicious and called the Housing Movement, who called us, and we arrived with a video camera. We enter the apartment already recording, and the supposed journalist is in trouble. What ensued was a sort of a scuffle. What surprised everybody that day was that it was a conflict which played out in the media. The infiltrator with his camera on one side, and us on the other with ours.*

The events of those days had their consequences. The female student who called the cameras in was threatened by the police. The following day the Ex-Emerson social center announced a press conference to deescalate the situation and avoid further risks to the student. During the conference they explained at length what had taken place in the apartment.

Cojote: *Following this even the most reluctant part of the old Antagonistic movement,[77] began to support our activities, overcoming their doubts that media work could be done differently.*

It is due to this event that the guys acquired the name 'Sgamati'.

Cojote: *Times were changing and we wanted to play the role of a hub for the movement by connecting various forms of activism. One of the first events we covered was the march against the NATO summit in Florence on the 24 and 25 May 2000. We sent updates via SMS directly from the streets to the web, publishing in real time.*

Sgamati started documenting local demonstrations. They took photos, shot videos, and wrote reports. The material was collected on the site, or rather on various sites, because there was still no single platform. Instead dedicated sites were opened for each big protest, such as that against the NATO summit. But the real innovation was the live reporting from the marches and the strategic use of cellphones, which had become affordable and spread like wildfire.

Sgamati was a constant presence at these local demonstrations, doing work that in a way preceded that of Indymedia – or at least is closer to what Indymedia would do in the future than to hacktivism. In essence, it was still a human approach to the web in the sense that one of them, Mille, was at the computer manually adding the text messages he received.

Pinke: *Back then, I helped with the site. I wrote the actual text, but not the HTML. Then with others who knew HTML, we put it online.*

---

77   Antagonist movement: The movements referred to in this instance are the Movimento Antagonista Fiorentino (MAF) and the Movimento Antagonista Toscano (MAT). The latter was active until around 2005.

And although more like an artisanal workshop than a hacklab, their method produced the desired results. People responded positively and they soon developed a reputation both locally and on the net.

Pinke: *Slowly interest built in what we're doing, at least in our circle of friends. Things grew through word of mouth, but we were always very cautious. It was a stealth operation. We had big discussions amongst ourselves, but we were only taking the first steps.*

Emboldened by the response from the community, the crew worked hard to improve their own practices, but while doing it, they soon had to deal with multiple problems, primarily the lack of a space in which to meet and do things together. They met in friends' offices. In the evening after everyone left, Sgamati would come in – so they could have access to a photo-copier, computers, and above all, an internet connection, which were still uncommon at home.

Beyond the technical problem of lacking an internet connection and not having a place to meet, there was also a shortage of resources: the video camera mentioned above had been borrowed so a still digital camera that could record short clips was often used instead.

Cojote: *There were always a few video cameras around, for example there was a psychology student who lent us one. But even if somebody lent us a video camera and we made a Hi8 tape, we still had to digitize it using a video capture card and so on…*

The solution to these problems began in June of 2000 with the squatting of the Cecco Rivolta, a farmhouse on the rolling hills of the Castello neighborhood.[78] Cecco not only solved the question of space, it also provided a supportive community for Sgamati and the other obsta-cles – the limited personnel, lack of resources and skill sets – became more manageable.

Pinke: *When the Cecco was squatted, there are those who actually squat and those like me, who showed up that day and stayed forever. From involvement with high school political collectives and small groups of friends, I went straight to the house and a whole new world opened for me. The others from Sgamati brought me here, they were living in the Cecco and were its techie soul. Since the beginning it has been a journey with all of them, one that continues to this day.*

Inside of the Cecco, Sgamati set up the 'Batcave', with the idea to make a computer lab-oratory open to all. It wasn't a real hacklab, but a space primarily dedicated to alternative media projects.

Pinke: *The Batcave wasn't a ghetto within the ghetto, but a meeting point that sparked many people's curiosity. Over the years it became a haunt for people who weren't part of either Cecco or Sgamati, people like Lobo, whom I met there.*

However, it's undeniable that some of the behavior appeared strange in the eyes of the other inhabitants.

Blanqua: *Pale skin, big bags under the eyes, long hair in a pony tail or 1980s style, dressed in black, born to sit hunched over a monitor. Favorite food: Kit Kats, Kinder chocolate bars,*

---

78   Castello neighborhood: Outlying neighborhood in northern Florence which borders on the industrial
      area of Sesto Fiorentino.

crisps, and Coca-Cola. I remember that once after thirty-three hours in front of their black screens with white text, one of us Cecco primitivists walked into the Batcave and asked, 'any of you guys want dinner?' And from their side, a growl, a smile, and then a symphony of clicks…

But let's return to cellphones and Mille seated in front of a computer. In September 2000, Sgamati organized minute by minute reporting from the first actual European anti-globalization protest – the countersummit in Prague against the meeting of the World Bank and International Monetary Fund.

Cojote: *Mille didn't come with us so we decided to do it like this: I would send a message like 'They're chasing us', or '… we turned the corner…' and he would add it to the web page. When he hadn't heard from us for too long, he called. Mille spent his nights in front of the computer but he did more than this: he called our parents and partners to keep them updated and went the extra mile to keep everyone calm and informed.*

Even if he received limited information about what happened to his friends, Mille was the Prague media center. During those days, their site competed with Radio Sherwood and with the continuing keystrokes of updates, arriving day and night, in the end, it epically overwhelmed ECN's bandwidth. This time Mille updated the site using a script written by Void, who would play a critical role in A/I.

Mille: *I'd already met Void in Bologna and we'd become friends.*

In fact, while Indymedia Italy had been born in Bologna, it hadn't yet established its own independence. The application had been submitted to the international committee allocating Indymedia domains, and was completed as part of the preparations for the protests against the OECD conference in Bologna between the 12 and 15 June, 2000.

Cojote: *Initially Void took care of the technical side and a member of Luther Blissett[79] managed the cultural part; he had been active internationally long before us and through his many contacts had obtained management of the domain, but had neither the structure, nor a project behind him. He didn't really want to post stuff on Indymedia, but rather to use the Indymedia brand to problematize the question of alternative media.*

At the time of the escapades of Sgamati in Prague Indymedia still didn't have the role it would carve out during the G8 in Genoa but no newspaper had a team that could possibly cover all the events taking place in a remote Czech city. Sgamati filled this gap. And as Hannibal Smith[80] would say, 'the plan came together'. It came together so well, that the earliest memory the Milanese have of the Florentines is tied to that mythical 'online newspaper'.

---

79   Luther Blissett: Luther Blissett was the first black English football player to transfer to an Italian team. Opposing fans subjected him to racial abuse. His name was then appropriated as a collective identity by groups dedicated to media criticism and urban experimentation. The art of the media hoax became a specialty of these groups as did the situationist-inspired practice of the derive – drifting through the city for the purpose of rediscovering its obscured possibilities.
80   Hannibal Smith: Leader of the A-Team, a fictional band of outlaw Vietnam veterans and vigilantes in pursuit of justice.

Cojote: *We weren't that interested in the technology itself so much as making news sites on movement events. We got on well together and felt good doing it. We were flattered by the immediate feedback. Although we had just appeared on the scene, we magically had an impact on the existing political context.*

After Prague, the Florentines developed the idea that they should bring the internet to the small political groups active in the region, spreading the tools for expression and communication – between themselves and with the larger world – to the social centers, squatted houses, collectives, groups both large and small – whoever needed it.

Pinke: *Between 2000 and 2001, I'm evolving and starting to think about power sharing beyond the immediate context. As a group we started to develop ideas – always about media – that pushed us beyond the mere documentation of marches. The political spaces and the movements, those who are active, need both the tools and the knowledge of how to use them – so they don't get fucked by them. There is also a transition from a phase of fascination with computers to the knowledge that like all tools, they can be used for good or for evil. There is the ripening of a deeply rooted concept which is at the base of A/I itself. A simple concept that you can use as a paradigm for many things. A/I was born for this purpose, to give people tools and to teach them how to use them.*

The name was already in place for the next stage of the project. The original nucleus of Sgamati had thought about it, and for the sake of precision, they came up with it during a car trip between the little town of San Gersolè in Chianti country and the banks of the Arno in Florence. Inasmuch as they had to 'invent' a name, the guys decided on 'Inventati' and decided not to decide where to put the accent, thus preserving the ambiguity between 'invent yourself' (*invèntati*) and 'the invented' (*inventàti*).

The name wasn't enough, obviously. The first thing was to provide a better structure for the group. The guys looked around, but among the groups already in existence there didn't seem to be one that could help them with such an ambitious plan. The hacklab, which they had always used, had now been reborn inside the CPA,[81] another social center, but this couldn't be regarded as a feasible framework. They had grown up in the CPA, knew how relationships were handled there and the culture was incompatible with what they wanted to do. Although the hacklab was a distinct group within the wider CPA, it overlapped extensively with the social center – the education projects, computer classes on free software, and an active artistic engagement made it a natural extension of it. In such a structured and rooted environment there was no place for a wildly different project like theirs, something new and open to all.

Cojote: *We knew exactly what we wanted. At that point we wanted to set up a server. We just didn't know how do to it. We needed someone who would teach us how to do it.*

Having discussed and consulted with the hacklab and ECN, they were put in touch with a lot of computing communities they could plausibly collaborate with, and they started to travel around Italy to meet with anyone with the skills to help them create an independent server. Whenever they could they visited a different city. In Puglia they formed important friendships, such as that with Phasa whom they met at a hacker meeting.

---

81 Centro Popolare Autogestito di Firenze Sud (CPA-FiSud): Historic social center in the Gavinana district south of the Arno in Florence; still active.

Cojote: *That summer Phasa joined us in Florence… I don't even remember what project we were working on at the time. Then he decided to stay.*

But despite traveling the length and breadth of Italy, it didn't come to anything, for the time being…

Bologna

Void is always singled out as one of the few who understood something about computers at the inception of A/I. And although this may come across as a bit extreme, the description is certainly appropriate if we look at the collective from the perspective of the Florentines with their lack of technical know-how, a lack which they compensated for with enthusiasm and endless creative resourcefulness.

But at the time Void was more skilled than most, if only because he was the last system administrator to join ECN.

Void: *I saw an episode of* Mediamente[82] *dedicated to ECN and the hacker underground on Rai 3. I was so struck by it that I wrote an email to the collective. Some time later, I moved to Bologna and decided to get in touch directly with Zombi_J from ECN and that's how we became friends.*

At the time, ECN was the movement's only alternative to commercial providers and Zombi_J was the point person for computer activism in Bologna. With him, Void started raising awareness regarding the use of digital tools and the advantages of free software in the radical left milieu, and his participation in the collective remained secondary initially. Introduced by Zombi_J, Void became part of Isole nella Rete at the end of 1999 and one of its system administrators in 2000.

Void: *I had always used computers but my skills were more focused on programming. With ECN, I learned about system administration.*

Broadband was scarce, and Void was almost always connected from the Grafton 9 bookstore – one of the very first places to offer internet-connected computers to the general public. The bookstore also had the particular characteristic of being a meeting point for Bologna's intellectual scene and played a far from marginal role during this period. Close to the Livello 57 social center,[83] it saw the birth of many projects, from the Bolognese section of the Luther Blissett project to Indymedia.

---

82   Mediamente: Television program broadcast on Rai 3 between 1994 and 2002, dedicated to raising awareness about computing and networks. The show also produced educational materials to accompany its broadcasts.
83   Livello 57 social center: Occupied social space in Bologna renowned for its activism in favor of a safer drug culture and decriminalization.

Void: *The relationship with the Florentines really started in 2000 during the period of anti-glo-balization*[84] *demonstrations in Italy. In May there are the actions against NATO in Florence and Forza Nuova,*[85] *a neo-nazi group, in Bologna, and in June the demonstration against the OECD, also in Bologna.*

The Bolognese were impressed by the role played by Indymedia in the coordination of the so-called 'People of Seattle'.[86] Thus, between the two planned demonstrations in their city, they busied themselves setting up the Italian version of the site. They went through the formal process required for participation in the Indymedia network and obtained the domain italy.indymedia.org just in time for the No OECD demonstrations – a week of workshops and other events organized together with the nascent Social Forums. At this point in time, Indymedia Italy was used as much to let people know what was happening in the city – like a calendar – as for independent reporting about what had happened. While today this may be taken for granted, back then it couldn't be. It was a continuous process of experimentation.

Void: *We had shot our first videos during the demonstration against Forza Nuova in Bologna. The Florentines had started their media activism in May, and they had seen what we had done and that the videos were online just a couple of hours later, so they asked for a meeting. That took place in Bologna in early June. At that point we were launching Indymedia and they expressed their interest. Next they came to the No OECD march. We immediately saw that we shared the same political bent and decided to stay in touch, also because we still didn't know exactly what to do with Indymedia.*

The initial proposition, at the suggestion of a member of the Luther Blissett project, was to make Indymedia seem like a colossus – a well-organized media organization. Indymedia Italy was in fact launched, for this occasion, with a lot of press releases and fake photos of the editorial staff sent to newspapers. After the No OECD demonstration, however, its potential as a tool turned out to be far more interesting: in addition to the infrastructure, the Americans released various technologies like a content management system (CMS), a program that managed content and automatically updated the site. This was similar to what Mille had done during Prague.

Void: *For the first time we saw a CMS... we didn't have any experience with online publishing or streaming... with their support we understood that it's not just a joke but something that can actually work.*

---

84   Anti-globalization movement: The demonstrations and forums held in opposition to the institutions of neo-liberal governance (G8, WTO, OECD, EU) were widely referred to as the anti-globalization movement until the turn of the 21st century. Thereafter the term became less popular. This was catalyzed in part by a fear that the movement might be seen as embracing nationalism and sympathetic to notions of a right/left alliance. Since then alternatives stressing the internationalist nature of the movement have become more popular, such as 'counter-globalization'.

85   Forza Nuova (FN): Neo-fascist organization founded by Roberto Fiore and Massimo Morsello. These two fled to the UK following the Bologna train station bombing of 1980 (85 killed, 200 injured), and did not return until the statute of limitations ran out on their offenses. Following their return FN began an energetic campaign to establish itself as a serious player on the far right, a process involving many provocative demonstrations in areas considered to be left-wing.

86   'People of Seattle': 'Il Popolo di Seattle' is the Italian way of referring to the coalition protestors present at the 1999 demonstrations against the WTO meeting. This is similar to the US formulation for that alliance: 'Turtles and Teamsters'.

After that first intense month of activity, Indymedia Italy became a discussion list about what to do with the project and remained so for the following months. Also in June, Void and the Florentines traveled together to the Hackmeeting which took place that year at the Forte Prenestino social center in Rome.[87] There they met the Milanese from LOA for the first time. Few remember any of this. But Void does, perhaps because his activism within ECN made it easier to read the map of social relations.

Void: *I already knew Blicero online via ECN, but I met him in person at the Hackmeeting in Rome.*

Between the Hackmeeting in Milan and the one in Rome, i.e. just over a year, the fundamental connections were made, allowing not only a generational handover, but also the birth of a veritable technical hothouse for the movement.

Caparossa: *I joined Autistici at the beginning because I knew the Milanese well after the Roman Hackmeeting. The year between the Hackmeeting in Milan in '99, and the one in Rome in 2000, I threw myself into the Hackmeeting list. I signed up a few days before going to Milan, and that's where I met everyone, a whole scene which still exists to some extent: Jaromil, Asbesto, the people from Catania, the Romans, Di Corinto and all that crowd. And that year there was the first contact between the Florentines and the Milanese (in fact the majority of the contact took place in Rome).*

At this point, the building blocks for Autistici/Inventati were all firmly in place.

First Meeting

Between the end of September and the beginning of October 2000, a meeting took place at the Bulk in Milan organized by Void. A kind of appeal had been broadcast into the ether of the Hackmeeting community. The idea was to meet and assess whether the circumstances were ripe for a further evolution of the political, technological, and communicative experiences then being produced in the hacklabs.

Blicero: *Void explained to us that Indymedia was already there, but that it was going to die if it wasn't used. Following this proffer, those present joined Indymedia en masse. What came into being would become the real Indymedia Italy.*

In particular, the discussion focused on the question of Indymedia and how to foster its potential.

Void: *For Indymedia this meeting was decisive. After the session at LOA, the Milanese, Florentines, and others joined the discussion list. In the space of a few months participation exploded and Indymedia took off.*

---

87   Forte Prenestino social center: Famous left libertarian squat in Southern Rome, originally built as a Napoleonic fort.

However, the session interests us in so far as it was also the first time the future protagonists of A/I met in a room together. That day, beyond the discussion about Indymedia, everyone present outlined their own projects. LOA, for example, expressed the need for more flexible digital tools to support the political life of movements.

Void: *ECN was the only alternative to commercial providers but it didn't offer sufficient services to the community – neither email, nor mailing lists – for which there was a growing demand. Above all there were significant technological limitations due to the fact that it was a small machine with very high hosting costs.*

This was confirmed by the Florentines, whose problem lay less in offering than accessing more agile services, given they were involved in at least ten different projects in their region.

Mille: *We talked about what we wanted to do and what they wanted to do, their approach to the web. The Milanese had thought about providing small sites on information security for the community. We didn't think about that, we were happy to meet them, because at the time it was also very difficult to meet people who understood what we were talking about. The people we interacted with politically only understood what we were talking about up to a certain point, even if they were very interested in our project.*

What emerged clearly from the discussion was the need to set up an infrastructure to permit further technological development.

Void: *Everyone needed services. We were all involved in the Hackmeeting scene and wanted an environment to experiment with, to think about, where we could learn things and put them into practice. And this is what the first year of Autistici/Inventati was to be about.*

From that day on, those present in Milan kept in touch for the purpose of developing Indymedia. And although they had wanted to keep their project separate from it, the two ended up sometimes overlapping and for many became indistinguishable: a synthetic activism expressed in combined gestures of participation.

Cojote: *We were always careful to keep the two things clearly separate, also because at the beginning many of us were part of both A/I and Indymedia.*

Afterwards, the two projects developed independently; Indymedia had an open structure and grew quickly, whereas A/I chose to remain a closed collective.

Both the LOA hackers and Inventati by default kept their politics under wraps, something which became characteristic of their presence within the political scene in the following years.

Cojote: *We wanted to distinguish ourselves from the old school, and this was all the more reason to not introduce ourselves as belonging to this or that political current...*

With the birth of the anti-globalization movement, the possibility of a more confrontational activism was in the air, and they wanted at all costs to avoid perpetuating the closures and mistrust that would prevent broad and bottom-up participation. If the mission was to spread the use of shared and effective tools, then it was necessary to do it in the most neutral way possible, avoiding any partisan logic which would discourage people from getting involved in the project of their own accord.

The Foundation

The next months were key to this story, but shedding light on them and establishing the facts does not prove easy – nor perhaps even useful. The historical account of Autistici is continuously undermined by the stories of Inventati, and our interviews often finish with such phrases as:

Cojote: *It was 2000, no, no, no, it was 2001, wait let's see… ah yes (sigh). It was May.*

Mille: *…It's possible that someone else remembers it better than me.*

Blicero: *… Alright I'm probably wrong, maybe the Florentines weren't at this meeting and instead came to the presentation in September.*

Anyway, the legend goes that immediately after the Indymedia meeting (which maybe they didn't even attend!) and encouraged by comrades from the hacklab, the Florentines got in touch with the Milanese once again. By now it was obvious that they had to ask these young Geeks of Good Hope for help.

Cojote: *At the Thursday night hacklab meetings, I'd made friends with Zeist from Piacenza,*[88] *and he'd already said good things about LOA. Then all of us, Ferry Byte, Sansa, TheWalrus, Leandro, and the others from the hacklab talked it over again and it seemed like the best solution. In the end, they mentioned us to the Milanese hackers as well.*

And so, in November of 2000, LOA received a mysterious email from Inventati. Communication proceeded solely by encrypted email and this explains the speed with which a meeting was organized in Milan in December.

Blicero: *I remember that Cojote or Mille asked for my PGP key to send me mail, claiming that they needed to tell me something top secret. It was: 'when can we meet?' So we organize this meeting super secret agent style… such a place, such a time, you will recognize me because I'm like so… then they arrive directly at LOA two hours late, in the General Lee – which was Cojote's rust bucket, it was legendary! – honking in via Niccolini while the pigs who were monitoring the squat watched us come down from LOA flabbergasted. It was absolutely ridiculous…*

And so LOA and Sgamati, or Autistici and Inventati, if you prefer, had a date at the new Bulk. They were joined by Void from Bologna. During the mythical dinner at the 'La Balena' pizzeria – the only factual element agreed on by all – the Florentines unveiled their seditious plan to the Milanese.

Blicero: *Basically, what they proposed was to create a server like ECN. The idea at the time was that it wasn't right that a single server provided services for the whole movement. The initial goal was to duplicate the experience of ECN and encourage others to do likewise. If there were ten thousand machines it would make it impossible to seize one and thereby block everyone's communications. Essentially the goal was to start a process of server multiplication. As we talked, it developed greater specificity, but that was the objective at the outset.*

---

88   Piacenza: Small city on the border between the regions of Emilia Romagna and Lombardy in Northern
      Italy.

Inventati needed not only technical help but also a collaborator who shared their motivations. And maybe because they didn't know how to set a server up but did know what to do with it, they wanted to offer the same opportunity to every politically active group in their region.

It would enable sites, mailing lists, and mailboxes to be set up with an ease almost equal to the speed at which new activists multiplied themselves, fragments of participation that urgently needed new means of coordination and interaction if they were to continue to exist.

Blicero: *For Inventati, the Florentine element had a more communications based approach to the web. Their main need was a space to host their publishing projects, from Sgamati to Copydown,[89] from Stampa Clandestina[90] – a newspaper meant to be pasted on the city's walls – to Spia la Spia[91] – a project to map security cameras in public spaces. But the proliferation of nodes was a fundamental strategic point for them too.*

The computer activists of the greater Milan area not only had the skills, they had the same ideas in the pipeline. Beyond the desire to experiment and put their skills into practice, the young hackers of LOA felt the need for a project of their own outside of ECN. Despite their contribution and some of them having been part of the original Milanese ECN collective, trivial generational issues made them guests – rather than protagonists – of that adventure.

Blicero: *For Autistici, they mostly focused on technological relationships and for the Milanese nerds, the big attraction was the opportunity to do something of our own. There was the desire to harvest and multiply the ECN experience and also to pay homage to it in some way, in synergy and not in opposition – indeed people from ECN were involved in the early stages of A/I.*

Autistici and Inventati immediately got along well and were in agreement on everything. During dinner, a lot of details were hashed out. Retracing Isole nella Rete's model, they decided to found a cultural association to manage the server and to give themselves a single name as an association – with each collective remaining separate.

Cojote: *They came from hacker circles and had autism as a practice – from there came the name Autistici. We brought with us the content of the Inventati project. From this union of two names we immediately baptized the associative project 'Investici', but our signature has always been A/I, from the idea of continuing to value both experiences.*

The double name is also due to the fact that the Florentines, not believing they would find good, resourceful people and with the desire to solidify their project, had already started a cultural organization and registered the domain Inventati.org.

Cojote: *In that period, we scoured Italy in search of tech support, but we also worked to become a real project regardless of what we had found.*

At the end of the meeting, they decided to put online a server that would be assembled in LOA. The Milanese willingly agreed to deal with the technological questions, which were

---

89   Copydown: See the dedicated chapter!
90   Stampa Clandestina: Underground Press.
91   Spia la Spia: Spy on the Spy.

their jurisdiction, while the Florentines brought the lists and sublists they managed, like the legendary A-TEAM, which hosted communication projects and followed the anti-globalization demonstrations before Indymedia.

On returning home, they had decided not only to construct the server and put it online, but also to meet again in Bologna at the next Indymedia Italy meeting.

Online

True to the principles of recycling, a server was assembled over the following months out of pieces of old hardware.

Pbm: *A bank was getting rid of equipment so we bought a server in 1998 for the symbolic price of 15 thousand lire (8+ US dollars at the time). Then we bought the hardware to expand it and recycled other hardware we already had, including a hard drive from my home computer...*

Once the mechanical part of the operation was concluded, Inventati and Void returned to Milan to configure the software.

Mille: *The 3 March 2001 is the day we declared: 'A/I now exists'. That's when we went to LOA for the server setup. On that occasion, everyone from our original Florentine group was there.*

It was a beautiful sunny Sunday. About ten people participated in the server configuration, with the least technical person on the keyboard – this was based on the idea that everyone should learn how to do everything. Obviously the situation was a bit chaotic, and a lot of time was lost deciding what's useful and what's not, whether to include the development tools[92] or not, and so on. Each proposal was discussed and executed only after everyone agreed to it. There was no plan, everything was done on the spot.

Pbm: *We wanted to offer the same services that were provided by the company I worked for, so I knew them well. The setup ought to have been a day's work but it took us longer because we decided to share the knowledge about how to do it. We thought it was important that everyone could see what was being done.*

The operation was performed with the usual care: everyone followed every step, the software packages were chosen one at a time – even if the Florentines still didn't understand very much to be honest.

Bomboclat: *But the differences between the two teams were overcome through a reciprocal trust, born between people who know each other and by default follow the same codes, like a certain level of paranoia regarding security and a certain attitude towards computers. These were the two things that bridged the gap with the Florentines.*

---

92   Development tools: These are programs used by software developers to create or debug applications. Examples would include compilers, source code editors, and debuggers.

And these were also the principal reasons for which the computer was conceived: on one side to free the users from strategies of social control and on the other to go back to the internet's original practice of free sharing. Not coincidentally, the first server was unanimously baptized Paranoia.

Bomboclat: *The server names are a story in themselves: Paranoia, Chernobyl, Astio, Rivolta. Then with the R+ Plan: Contumacia, Latitanza…*[93]

From the beginning, A/I didn't take themselves that seriously. And how could it be otherwise, given that the execution of their diabolical plan was dotted with epic-absurd episodes, such as the guys locking themselves out of the server on the second day of its existence with the command:

```
iptables -A INPUT -p all -s ! 127.0.0.1 -j DROP
```

rendering the computer autistic and shut off from the world.

Pbm: *Ginox had taken charge of the development of network security, so he was studying iptables. The following morning, he goes to LOA, begins to work and enters the famous command, mistakenly prepending it with a '!', inverting it. He wanted to permit complete access from the computer to the computer, so that all internal services could communicate between each other. Except that he forgot an exclamation mark and, instead of permitting it, he denied access to everything that didn't come from the machine. Practically the machine could only communicate with itself. There isn't a more autistic server than that… We liked it so much that we made a t-shirt out of it!*

With the idea of acknowledging the two diverse personalities of the collective – the Milanese and the Florentine, the technical and the communicative – both domains were hosted on the machine: Autistici.org and Inventati.org.

Bomboclat: *In this sense Autistici/Inventati is born as Janus…*[94]

… such way started a bipolar digital adventure: the two groups sharing the space and time of a single server, each maintaining their own specificity.

Alieno: *We immediately attempted to respect a logical division whereby all hacking projects ended up on the Autistici.org domain whilst all cultural and activism projects went on Inventati, even if due to specific requests we often broke the rules. The home pages had different graphic design until 2004, when we changed the site and unified the two pages.*

Starting in April 2001, the computer was online. As distinct from ECN's server, which paid a provider for hosting, Paranoia was on the net for free. A collocation spot and guaranteed bandwidth for the newly born cultural association's server were quickly negotiated with Pbm's workplace. This arrangement was no small detail as the whole operation would otherwise have been prohibitively costly.

---

93 The servers' names roughly translate as: Paranoia, Chernobyl, Grudge, Revolt, Contumacy, Life on the Run.
94 Janus: The ancient Roman god of beginnings and transitions. He looked simultaneously towards both the future and the past, and thus is depicted with a face on both sides of the head.

Pbm: *The first, second, and third computer were hosted by the company I worked for. I had obtained this collocated server as a bonus and a favor. It was a company I knew well, I trusted them, and they trusted me. It being understood that the server was my responsibility, I could handle difficult situations such as when the police came asking for data... something that happened repeatedly.*

Training

Initially A/I was basically a list, a permanent decision-making body. The main activity was talking. And it was a crucial moment both because the two groups had to get to know each other and because of the enormous technical differences between them.

Pinke: *In the early period of A/I there were a bunch of discussions, a lot was written, an infinite amount of mail was sent. We Florentines in particular wrote so much and they teased us about it! We had the longest, deepest meetings, because clearly we had a lot of things to discuss. We had the impression that a lot would depend on these decisions. We were laying the foundation for a project that shouldn't die after two years, but survive, and each service was chosen with the strategic view of opening it to the public and gaining people's trust. A lot of discussions. Nice and constructive, but so many!*

They were very careful, especially in deciding how to work together. For example, after having explored various options, they decided to have a single mailing list for all questions: technical, political, and organizational.

Pinke: *We didn't want to create two separate internal flows, separating the technical and non-technical people, so we decided to have a single list and to try and bridge the gap so that those of us who were more political could become more technical and vice versa. At the beginning the list was a mess. I kept all the emails, in particular those from Pbm, which were filled with detailed technical explanations of how to configure various services. I studied them and tried and bring myself up to speed. I started from zero and only touched the machines if someone checked what I did.*

The distinctive trait of the new association was in fact that everyone could do everything. Everyone had the same privileges on the computer, everyone was 'root' – that is a superuser, or administrator.

Pinke: *They offered me shell access like they did to everyone who joined the collective. I refused it saying I didn't know enough yet, and when I did understand I would ask for it. In the meantime I tried to overcome my limits, studying, asking for advice and explanations. The training took place limited by an awareness that we, the 'non-techies', shouldn't slow the collective down too much and they, the 'techies', must do a good job explaining what they were doing so as not to leave any of the less experienced people too far behind. In time we arrived at an equilibrium and we were able to keep it.*

The difference in skill was seen as a resource. Those who didn't initially have sufficient confidence in their computer skills studied, while devoting themselves to managing the info@ mails and responding to users and/or contacting projects from local political groups and offering them mailboxes, web pages, or the digitization and archiving of materials.

Caparossa: *It wasn't necessary to be a super hacker, because at the time the mindset was: everybody should do everything. Everyone had to make a minimum effort to understand what they were doing. The documentation we made for ourselves became public documentation in part. I read everything and learned a number of things that otherwise I would have had to learn from books. And besides, I learned to think before hitting return, and that's no small thing.*

The acceptance of different skills as a resource didn't mean that people didn't strive to overcome the limits such differences usually imply. It was assumed that those who were more knowledgeable would manage the server, but the members of the collective continued to teach one another with the idea that everyone could participate, and also because an ability to contribute at the technical level meant sharing the drudge work.

Cojote: *The Milanese had an impressive capacity to place value on the training process in and of itself. Today I can say that was probably key to a bunch of things. We could have brought the energy, but we didn't have the same capacity for the systematization of our practice... we proceeded off the cuff, if something interested us, we did it. I remember Pbm and Blicero, they had an incredible dedication and were captivating about topics that were unknown and difficult for us... and I studied computer science in Pisa. I may have learned the method there, but the things that are still useful today in my work, I learned at LOA.*

To allow the less prepared members to at least activate mailboxes, TxO wrote the first graphical interface, bypassing the technical steps, allowing anyone to administer the daily bureaucracy.

Caparossa: *There was this little panel made by TxO that was a shell, but an interactive one. He had written the most beautiful little scripts in Perl. If you wanted to create a list, you entered the command; you entered this colored interactive shell, there was a help command that told you the meaning of each color, then you entered the commands 'create list', 'create website', 'create mail'...*

Among the less technical people was Mille, who had studied Unix but never felt really competent, so he dedicated himself to responding to activation requests and building relationships with users. An incredible job and certainly no small task, so much that when the quantity of requests became maddening, someone proposed a self-help forum.

Caparossa: *Another thing that was said at the beginning is that we wanted a relationship with those using our services. We didn't want to be a service provider for the movement. And so in the beginning info@autistici.org and info@inventati.org were services operated by humans, where you talked with people. When they asked you for a mailbox, a mailing list or a site, you said: 'Yes, but why?' It wasn't an automatic service, it was one human who responded to another human, and we interacted.*

The list obviously helped with coordination, but regular meetings were held to give a shared structure to the management of the server. As the first meeting for the server installation was in LOA, the second meeting was held at the Cecco in Florence. Visit after visit, the Milanese made a fundamental contribution to the construction of the Batcave.

Mille: *It was Pbm who did the first Debian installation, and while he worked he explained everything that was happening to us. It was the most interesting thing ever.*

LOA gave tech support and simultaneously taught the Florentines a great deal. To give an idea of the situation, Sgamati had no knowledge of Linux except for some basics, and with the idea of giving away tools, they distributed through the Copyleft project a CD with cracked versions of proprietary software, as well as a file with installation instructions and codes to install them.

Alieno: *Until they forced me to create a Linux partition for A/I, I was a Windows user…*

These were intense months. With A/I, Inventati started a journey to independent computing, although the difference between 'techies' and 'reporters' would persist for a long time.

Direct Communication

In the early period of collaboration the individual elements of A/I changed in form, but not in substance. Everyone continued their own activities in their cities. In Florence, what they did differently was give out email addresses from the new domain, engaging in a work of widespread dissemination.

Pinke: *Mille made it a personal crusade. He opened hundreds of mailboxes and mailing lists for existing political organizations. For our part we discussed how to bring A/I into the real world and did it by tabling at events and painting graffiti. Our work was manic, making photocopies on top of photocopies – that's what they were used to at the Cecco – and giving out A/I leaflets, Kriptonite, or floppies by Strano Network while tabling. We went to university parties, to the festivals organized by L'Unità,[95] wherever there were people. When the free photocopy period was over, to continue giving away the material we taxed ourselves, and later we made our own merchandising: t-shirts, stickers, pins, and sweatshirts to finance it. Mille meanwhile approached everyone and convinced them to open an email account. He did all this work and opened an infinite number of accounts. On top of that, he opened lists for collectives and visited everybody to explain that mailing lists were a coordination tool, and since these tools proved to be really useful, at some point collectives asked us to create them.*

Inventati had to really pressure the political groups, the social centers, squatted houses, and collectives to use these new technologies. These new means of communication were met with huge distrust, starting at the Cecco itself. It wasn't only the group's base of operations, but as it was populated by the youngest activists, it was supposed to represent a gathering of the most open minded.

Blanqua: *It seems impossible, but at the beginning many of us didn't even know how to switch on a computer. Yes, the computer: the enemy. That's how it was. I remember the work to create the Batcave and that Pilar, my dog that I'd just gotten at the time, had decided to shit only in there. And in my heart I thought she was right. What kind of room should only have computers in it?*

---

95   *L'Unità*: Italian newspaper founded by Antonio Gramsci; it was originally the official newspaper of the Italian Communist Party (1924-1991). The 'Festa de *L'Unità*' is an annual event which used to finance the newspaper. In Tuscany and Emilia Romagna these festivals are especially widespread and significant.

In practice, only those who came from the hacklabs or knew ECN understood A/I's message. For the majority of people, the talk about privacy, anonymity, and technology was still incomprehensible.

Pinke: *It must be said that email wasn't the indispensable tool it is today. The internet and tools for it were starting to spread, but they were still something for the elite.*

In such a situation Inventati's answer was the elaboration of a broad communication strategy, something that created curiosity, something that, in substance, was closer to the people in the collective. To do it, the decisive push came from the squatters of the Cecco.

The group that was squatting the Cecco contained a strong component inspired by situationist[96] practices, which gave the Cecco its second name 'GSA' ('*ghetto super giovani antinoia*').[97] It was from their ideas of *détournement*[98] that Inventati devised their guerrilla advertising campaigns to publicize themselves locally.

Cojote: *At the Cecco we learned a lot from one other... the idea for our graffiti came from our situationist friends. It was them who told us how to do things and how to communicate with people.*

The two groups at Cecco weren't cut from the same cloth and in many cases came from very different cultural backgrounds. Nevertheless they had known each other for a while and had united in pulling off a series of actions and provocations – from an improvisational play staged in a bus to the squatting of the farm house that would become the Cecco.

Pinke: *Initially we had to take stock of one another: on one side we brought the computers into the Batcave, constructing this dark, shadowy environment; on the other, they were in the garden, bucolic... in brief, we had to find a way to understand each other. One time they even did a march inside the Batcave singing 'Playstations, pigs, and cops, we'll wipe you out from the Cecco Rivolta!*[99]

The Cecco was a lively political experiment, twenty people working out a way to live together. There were even 'internal factions': the cinephiles, the technocrats, the philosophers. However, after the first session/clash, the squatters got to know each other better and share their mutual passions and interests.

Blanqua: *Whether you wanted it or not, at a certain point the Batcave became real. Imagine about fifteen people who have never been to a web page, never been on the internet. And then suddenly someone shows up and explains to you how to turn on a computer, how to*

---

96   Situationist: The Situationist International was a group active between 1958 and 1969, predominantly in continental Europe. Whilst it is often associated today with the cultural avant-garde, it was actually a social revolutionary organization which sought to overcome capitalism and end the separation between life, art and politics. Its best known exponents were Guy Debord and Raoul Vaneigem.

97   'Super Young Anti-Boredom Ghetto': A pun on CSA, which means 'centro sociale autogestito', or self-managed social center.

98   *Détournement*: the practice of re-purposing well known symbols, characters or narratives for subversive purposes.

99   A play on the 80s Autonomen chant: 'Eroina, fascisti e polizia, dai nostri quartieri vi spazzeremo via' (Heroin, Fascists, Cops, we'll wipe you out of our neighborhoods!).

turn it off, how to navigate the internet... but guys, everything comes at a cost. You couldn't possibly open the sloooow mail from Inventati on Windows: it would have been too easy! Windows had become the new super-enemy for the Super Young Anti Boredom Ghetto, we had to learn how to love our server and above all Linux, that great unknown. Regarding Linux I mainly remember Ilnonsubire, like when you're in elementary school and you have to learn Alessandro Manzoni's poem Il cinque maggio[100] by heart; he taught me how to download my mail. Mutt, ping, pong – when I recall them, I feel like a professional hacker. But what happened was really a miracle. Inventati, also for someone like me who today still labors to understand the mysteries of the internet, was a child of a collective organism. I didn't really know what it was all about, but it was mine too.

And following the suggestions of the other Cecco squatters, Inventati 'launched' a graffiti campaign, designed to appear on walls both highly visible and hard to reach – in fact some lasted five or six years before someone took the trouble of painting over them. To do it they climbed up and down to reach bridges, overpasses and the most unlikely places.

At first they only said 'Inventati'. The idea was to create anticipation and many people started to wonder what this word meant, how it was pronounced, who could be behind it. Afterwards they started to write 'Inventati.org'. This bizarre operation brought the attention of some local journalists, given that, at the time, it was very strange to see an internet address on a wall.

The idea of graffiti for an underground media launch had been tested during the protests against the war in Kosovo, when the city was plastered with a peace sign with 'WHY?' next to it. Among the significant places chosen for this inscription was the scaffolding that at the time covered the facade of the famous Basilica of Santa Croce.[101]

Cojote: *The trick of direct communication lies in the pervasiveness of the message. In this case the idea was that every tourist that passed in front of Santa Croce would take a photo, it would circulate at such a level that it would achieve its effect. As for the writing 'Inventati' we wanted to create anticipation and we did. The domain was bought before we put it on a server and was virtually empty. We wanted to attract people. The curiosity it provoked helped us, but what counted above all was the fact that we were always in the right place at the right moment during important events, when things happened. That's how we rooted ourselves in the territory. The thing that worked is really that we tried to be everywhere.*

A/I's foundation and putting the independent server online, the graffiti campaign, their constant presence in social spaces, and Mille's personal crusades were all elements that when put together exceeded all expectations. Within a few months, the movement started to understand the meaning of the project. When they were tabling there was a line to get passwords and instructions for a new or first email address on little handwritten pieces of paper.

Mille: *Often we made @inventati email addresses, but it was also possible to make @autistici addresses – the form was the same, but it was hard explaining this dual possibility! Until we opened the other domains, we would advise one or the other depending on the type of project, but after all, people in Florence in general would always ask to have an @inventati email, because it was cool, we were well known, etc, etc. Vice versa in Milan they asked for @autistici.*

---

100   *Il cinque maggio*: Poem by A. Manzoni about the death of Napoleon Bonaparte on Saint Helena. It is taught in Italian schools.
101   Basilica of Santa Croce: Famous church in Florence situated on an expansive square of the same name.

Indymedia

On one side A/I was based on the assumption that new technologies were acquiring a dangerously invasive role in people's life, and the first years were spent on a campaign for the use of digital tools which kept the user in control, like Linux. On the other, however, A/I also shared a literary intuition that communication, augmented by the same technologies, was starting to carry more weight at events and thus it was necessary to concern themselves with alternative media, and not just computing.

Bomboclat: *It was during those years that the figure of the media activist emerged. Politics and technology merged, thanks to the glue of the digital possibilities. From the idea of producing alternative media we switched to the idea of being the media. Defining propaganda as everything that comes from television, we created our own concept of media.*

A/I was a sort of happy meeting between skills and content, an experience that reflected the historic transition when technology and communication merged into the wider cognitive area known today as information technology. In the months in which the collective formed, almost every participant was found to be also involved with Indymedia,[102] an information source meant to be both organized and shared.

Blicero: *Indymedia had a first phase in which it was essentially managed from Bologna as part of a hoax, then it was a large network of people based in the hacklabs. This same network, that later that gave life to A/I, joined Indymedia on the understanding that communication managed in this way reduced the capacity for the hegemonic control by specific subjects, and Indymedia was a tool that could be used equally by everyone, in contrast to radio, TV, or newspapers. This was possible because of how the tool itself worked. It could be done – it was a goal that could be pursued. That is more or less what we did.*

---

102 Indymedia: Although Indymedia.org debuted in December 1999 during the Seattle protests against the WTO, its software was developed in Australia the previous summer for use during the global 18 June protest against the G8. This system was called 'Active' and it enabled what was called 'open publishing' where users could write and upload their news directly onto a continuously updated web page. The events of 1999 took place against the background of increased international coordination between activists protesting the most visible institutions of the neoliberal consensus: EU, G8, WTO, etc. This new internationalism and attention to trade questions had been catalyzed by the Zapatistas in Chiapas, Mexico. They brought their supporters together in a series of gatherings, or *encuentros*, held from 1996 onwards, out of which emerged People's Global Action (PGA), a key organizational node for the anti-globalization movement. The Zapatista *encuentros* also facilitated a fresh round of coalition building; their broad appeal brought together many groups without any history of collaboration. These new connections were visible in Seattle and described in the media as an alliance of Teamsters and Turtles. The Indymedia.org domain was registered and set up to provide live coverage of events on the streets in Seattle. It was such a success that the site was maintained and other regional sites began to spring up all over the world. Some time later it developed a process whereby prospective local operators had to apply and be approved by existing participants, as there was a fear that the brand had become so powerful that its use required some level of management.

For Indymedia, the testing ground was the anti-globalization demonstrations, the beating heart of internationalism[103] in this period. But it built on the many local efforts from the people in Bologna, Sgamati, and those organized in Naples by the Rete Campana – the network of the anti-globalization movement in the region of Campania.[104]

ManO: *In March of 2001, there was the No Global Forum here in Naples. The event opposed the eponymous summit held by the OECD in the city. For the first time, we started to contemplate confusedly the use of different supporting technologies. For example, we registered a series of domains that could actually be from the OECD, like globalforum.it. Probably at the time there wasn't yet a requirement on the part of these economic institutions to create a site for every event. We found this domain and guys from various social centers said to me, 'Look, we got this domain, we can create the site and at the same time we want to organize a media center'.*

On the 17 March 2001, during the demonstration against the OECD's Global Forum on E-government in Naples, there was heavy fighting between police and protesters. The violence against the protesters – who were beaten throughout the course of the march, and suffered reprisals in back alleys and torture in police stations – was splashed across the front page of the newspapers.

ManO: *The No Global Forum didn't go very well, but we did come up with the idea of a media center. At the time nobody in Naples talked about Indymedia; some were very distrustful whereas to others it just seemed like total crap... however it was the first attempt to do something of that kind. Basically we put computers on a network with a set of free software tools and made them available to everybody. The media center was set up at the S.K.A. squatted laboratory and was the first time I participated in such a thing, where we tried to make this technology available for a 'cause'. At the same time, I started to make contact with other Italian political groups on IRC.*

The events of Naples showed that the level of the political conflict between police and anti-globalization protesters had notably increased. On the media front, they attracted the attention of half the world's press, above all due to the episodes of violence where people were indiscriminately beaten in the street. But on the digital front these events illustrated that the movement had a common need to publish and circulate photos, audio, and video produced by protesters, in a way that was less confusing, more efficient, shared, and at a national level.

The tool to do it was already there, it was Indymedia Italy. The tech support was there too, it was the hacker community.

---

103 Internationalism refers in general to the desire for coordination and cooperation on a basis of rejecting national chauvinism. In the case of social movements it generally refers more to the idea of working class internationalism; that capitalism is a global system and that workers must unite internationally if they are to defeat it. The most famous early manifestation of this thinking was the Zimmerwald Conference held by socialists in Switzerland in 1915, where participants from all over Europe came together to repudiate WW1 as an imperialist war with which the working class should have no truck.

104 Campania: Region surrounding Naples in the south of Italy.

The Joy of Doing

As we've already recounted, the Autistici/Inventati collective was born from the meeting of two groups: the Milanese and the Florentines. And there was Void from ECN, who lived in Bologna and had his hands in Indymedia Italy. However, it wasn't just these elements that merged to form A/I.

Bomboclat: *There were the Turinese, who started the Hackit99 channel with us in preparation for the Hackmeeting in Milan: Elettrico, Takazawa, etc. LOA called the Turinese la succursale, the branch office. It was a bunch of people around El Paso social center,[105] Radio Black Out, and ECN, who had participated in the Hackmeeting. At the beginning there were also some people from Freaknet and others who came and went, like Lechuck. Lobo had always been there, getting to Autistici/Inventati through Strano Network and the hacklab at the CPA Firenze Sud.*

This first period saw the story of the collective intersect with many other elements of the digital world and cross-pollinate with people from a wide variety of political groups, generally connected in some way to the world of the Hackmeetings, computer labs or self-managed spaces.

Bomboclat: *It was a period of great ferment and Autistici reflected this effervescence somewhat. There were people from Milan, Bologna and Turin, but also from the other cities where there were hacklabs or such...*

During the first period, references to biblical plagues appeared repeatedly – the death of the firstborn, water turning into blood, the plague of locusts – an imagination grounded in the catastrophic and apocalyptic taken from science fiction, cyberpunk, and the need to establish an ironic distance from their own computing disasters.

Alieno: *They were really the catchphrases of the Hackmeeting list – that at the time was hosted on the servers of kyuzz.org. The plague of locusts[106] literally stuck, turning up on the stickers and t-shirts we made for the 2004 Hackmeeting in Genoa and then into the name of the blog we added in 2005 to integrate the news section of our official website.*

Once the server was online, it was decided not to emphasize the services offered, as much as the technical aspects of the whole operation. Technical considerations included, and still include, the fact that A/I does not keep logs of its users' activity, promotes the use of cryptography, offers an anonymous remailer service and publishes how-tos about online communications privacy.

Shah: *The use of cryptography online made sense to me in this period, and I was interested and enjoyed it. Putro, who was our GPG teacher, came to LOA from outside of Milan and put up with the hassle of teaching because being there was so much fun. We immediately started to fool around with cryptography, but only a bit later, when the technical difficulties were dealt with, was CryptoKitchen born. In practice, we started a mailing list where you signed*

---

105 El Paso social center: Uncompromising anarchist squat and venue in Turin. Despite being called a social center, they describe themselves as 'neither central nor social'.
106 The plague of locusts: The Italian word for 'locusts' is 'cavallette', which is also the name of A/I's blog: cavallette.noblogs.org.

up and learned cryptography by exchanging recipes. The next step was a website that had a database with the recipes exchanged on the list, also encrypted. We did it particularly with Manhattan, while TxO was behind creating the nuts and bolts of the submission process...

The 'technical' aspects had their roots in ECN. However, in contrast with ECN, the young Autistici hackers did not have an almost bureaucratic need to negotiate every step. ECN was a product of its environment and above all the years in which the movement had decisively split. So its policies had to reflect the many different sensibilities of its participants.

Meetings in ECN happened between very different people with very different politics while participation was a great responsibility: every service request, every single mailing list, had to be judged and voted upon. They always had to clearly understand who was responsible for the new user or mailing list.

Blicero: *The big difference between A/I and ECN (which we copied a lot) is that we created mailboxes and hosted websites, lists and chat services also for smaller groups that weren't of national significance. It's worth considering that at that moment in time they had just started to use these tools. The main difference regarding internal organization was the sharing of power – everybody had root on the first A/I server, while at ECN only two people had it. What we did was insane from a technical standpoint, but it had a political meaning for us.*

With time, the sharing of power became an intrinsic characteristic of the list, a feature that prompted much food for thought on the experience of A/I.

Azi-1: *I read the list with great interest because I immediately appreciated the fact that we were a community based on a shared working method. Perhaps in this moment, it wasn't openly said, but the idea that we were making decisions based on informal consensus, and seeing that it worked, was really exciting for me.*

Besides, LOA had attracted the Milanese hacker underground – a really diverse group with many people who were more interested in free software and digital rights than the political actions of local groups. This is one of the reasons why the collective was less selective from the start about who they provided services to than ECN, because its members didn't carry the old, heavy baggage of the movement.

Shah: *I had joined ECN, was a part of LOA, and experienced the birth of A/I as a part of the increasing aggregation of people around our hacklab, which kept widening its scope and drawing in new people and projects. It was normal that at a certain point something larger than ECN and Isole nella Rete would be born. However A/I was something new and not just an evolution of ECN, really because the Florentines brought an aspect that was, let's say, humanistic, which was actually lacking at LOA. It was something interesting. I believe that LOA would have collapsed in on itself if it had been built only around the technical aspect. Putting the two elements together, Inventati guaranteed this experience would survive longer.*

In a certain sense, the Florentine group had formed in a more traditional way and, at the moment of contact with the Milanese, was experiencing a transition to technical proficiency as a political necessity. The people from Inventati came from the student collectives, social centers, and squatted houses. For them the need for a server and anonymous services were natural supports to their political activity. It's worth citing for example the project *SpiaLaSpia*, which perhaps best represents the commitment of the collective.

Pinke: *There was a map under construction of security cameras in Florence. The idea was born from looking at a similar map of San Francisco, which at the time was fiercely discussed because it was a way to bring home to people the magnitude of urban surveillance. At the time it still made sense to talk about privacy (or at least we saw it that way), and Rodotà,[107] the Italian ombudsman for the protection of personal data, created strict rules aimed at limiting the invasiveness of CCTVs. It was the golden age of 'friendly cameras'.[108]*

Spialaspia.org was conceived as an open publishing site, you filled out a form, entered the camera's geographic location and technical specs, and whether the camera was an invasion of privacy (for example: 'it should only cover the ATM but instead it takes in the whole street'). The motto, paraphrasing the well-known graphic novel *Watchmen*, was 'who watches the watchmen?' Unfortunately the watchmen didn't like this initiative very much and some people ended up under investigation because photographs of security cameras were found in their homes.

Pinke: *In hindsight, in view of the events of the 11 September, the era of Facebook and the voluntary renunciation of privacy, this all looks silly and maybe a bit naive. It served, however, to make us understand the world we were living in and the direction it was moving.*

In a certain sense, the Milanese were on the same path but coming from the opposite direction. Autistici was formed out of a shared passion for technology and, with the birth of A/I, they were now getting closer to local political activity.

Blicero: *In Milan we experienced an evangelical phase, a hardcore activism. You were always going around doing something. The situation was fervid, going all over the place and suggesting IT tools, trying to convince people and groups to adopt these new methods of communication.*

And in the confrontation with the real world, Autistici realized that the machinery they had put in place worked well enough.

Bomboclat: *There was synergy between the spread of these technologies and developing mutual trust because we were all engaged in building things and people saw that when you said something, you did it.*

Over just a couple of months the different parts of the new collection fused together through the joy of doing: they wanted to spread the tools described in Kriptonite as far as possible, to make it possible for everyone and to reach a critical mass.

Shah: *In practice A/I retraced the development arc of LOA where once the machines were set up, the question became: 'Now that we have this nice toy, what do we do with it?' And once again, everybody had contributed in their own way.*

---

107 Stefano Rodotà: Constitutional lawyer, one-time data commissioner, and candidate for the Italian presidency in 2013.
108 Friendly camera: 'Friendly' here is a reference to the government's propaganda for surveillance – cameras are 'friendly' in that they 'protect against crime'.

Hackmeeting in Catania: A Train Load of 486s

Meanwhile, after getting the server online in April, the first efforts at digitization began to appear. Among them, the Primo Moroni Archive[109] – a real coup for the collective, which would make Primo Moroni's phrase 'Share knowledge, without installing power' its motto.

Bomboclat: *We began putting sites online, starting from the contacts we had before we got on the web, that we inherited from our previous work in the area. The Primo Moroni Archive was ready by June, when we presented the project in Catania.*

A/I was in fact officially unveiled in June of 2001 at the Hackmeeting, held that year in Catania at the Auro social center and the Freaknet Medialab.

Bomboclat: *For the collective's debut we'd chosen what we considered the most worthy location. In Catania we had the most beautiful week, mystical, unforgettable! I did my first workshop with C1cc10. It was just Linux on a set of floppy discs, but for us it was something fantastic that everyone had to be told about, also because we thought, 'if we present it, maybe somebody listening will join the project and it will become something bigger'. As young nerds we had developed the idea that by talking about it with other hackers, maybe it would change. And actually there was a lot going on at the Hackmeeting that year...*

For members of the collective that year's Hackmeeting lasted more than a week rather than three days, and turned out to be a genuinely rich experience.

Bomboclat: *We went down to help out Freaknet and get the place ready and then we wanted to meet all the people whom we'd read online but still not met. We went by train, and took up almost an entire car, because we brought our classroom with us, in the sense that we'd dismantled it, packed it up, brought it to Catania and reassembled it at Auro. Imagine thirty, forty people with their cargo of 486s... There were, it seemed, twenty something workstations, that we left down there because LOA already had a project under way to move to Pentium 1s that, please note, had already been around for six years at that point.*

It was therefore an event that went beyond the presentation of the project itself and above all helped the hackers get to know each other, to have a first confirmation that A/I really and truly existed.

Ginox: *We came from Turin, we left straight from Radio Black Out's festival to Milan and then on to the deep south together with LOA. Before the TAV made traveling by rail unaffordable and night trains were canceled, you could cross Italy on the most uncomfortable trains, but at least they cost little and you weren't forced to sit next to loser managers and salesmen in*

---

109 Primo Moroni Archive: Primo Moroni (1936-1998) was a key figure of the revolutionary and countercultural milieu in Milan for over forty years. An autodidact, writer, and professional dancer, he opened a bookshop, Calusca, in 1971 which became a faucet for political and cultural heterodoxy, including the introduction of beat and hippie literature that would quickly have a significant impact in Italy. His book *L'orda d'oro*, co-authored with Nanni Ballestrini, remains the definitive account of the revolutionary movement in Italy in the '60s and '70s. The archive contains his personal collection of books, tracts, and ephemera amassed over those years and has been supplemented by the addition of other private collections.

their suits and ties. There I met the whole collective for the first time. Before I had the wrong idea about who belonged to which group. In Catania there was a large meeting in the tents in Auro's courtyard. A beautiful glimpse cut in half by a convent, a funny situation, because in the morning we had breakfast with an interactive class on blasphemy. The Hackmeeting at the Auro was important because the collective had a chance to focus on a concrete purpose: fix the social center's bathrooms to be able to host the HackIt and upgrade the electrical system. This is why Elettrico came with us from Turin and did his best. Also for the first time I did something more playful with the whole merry band; to be precise we went to the beach for a swim. At this point the presentation of A/I was almost unnecessary, anyway it was held in what seemed to be the rooms of a gym, with a ring in the middle. It was a sort of nativity scene, with the newly born server in the manger and all our friends had come to have a look and make funny faces at it. There were more people on the stage than in the audience, everything was buzzing. Anyway after Catania, we started to exist for real. Many people signed up for the list even if they didn't do anything and left a year later. My view is that A/I was a child of a certain cultural soil, of a wide community, with borders which were neither definite nor definable, but if you were within them you knew what they were talking about. It was our attempt to structure something starting out of the ideas that circulated in that environment.

Those days in Catania left a strong imprint in the memories of the hackers of Autistici, all the more so because they fit in a sequence of similarly intense experiences that in hindsight proved decisive for the future of A/I.

Bomboclat: *But after the Hackmeeting the journey continued. First we went to visit Asbesto from Freaknet in Palazzolo Acreide, Sicily,[110] then we went on to an appointment with history, in Genoa.*

Genoa

After the events in Naples, the repression against the movement underwent another violent escalation. At the European summit meeting in Gothenburg, a boy was shot by police firing 'into the air' and fell into a coma.

In June, with the fear of more street battles, the World Bank cancelled its annual conference on economic development which was to be held in Barcelona.

In July, with the G8 in Genoa just round the corner, there were different positions within the movement regarding how to manage and participate in the countersummit. Also amongst the techies in A/I based in the greater Milan area there was a lot of skepticism about getting involved in the organization of the media center.

Blicero: *When the G8 in Genoa came about, the general position is that we shouldn't take part, that it's a trap. This position was shared by everyone. But if you don't go, what do you do? Go to the beach? And so I decided to go. Then I got everyone from LOA and the Hackmeeting involved. In the end everybody got involved.*

---

110 Palazzolo Acreide, Sicily: A small town in the province of Syracuse. After the eviction of CSOA Auro in Catania, this town's 'poetry hacklab' briefly hosted the Freaknet hacklab.

In fact, some people did go to the beach, but only to show their dissent through an absolutely brilliant joke. The action was called 'Everyone to Varazze'.[111]

Caparossa: *At a certain point in the spring of 2001, in the middle of the organizational build-up to the G8 in Genoa, some of us anarcho-cyclists produced a document with a few other people. And we – myself, Alieno and Tapiro – put up a site called 'Turn Off G8' which essentially asked 'why should we walk into a trap? Instead of walking into the maw of these pieces of shit, to have a fight where they'll kill us… it's not only the Italian State, it's the G8, they're all there, why the fuck are we going there to get beaten up?' And we were optimistic. Let's tell them to fuck off and throw a great three day rave in Varazze. And in fact the slogan was 'Everyone to Varazze'. In Varazze they shat a brick because fifty something people really did show up and found the city militarized. But in the end family is family, so in July 2001 we all went to Genoa.*

For the counter-summit, the province and city of Genoa made available, respectively, a hundred computers and two buildings: the Diaz/Pertini and Pascoli schools. The activists involved in the communications group of the Genoa Social Forum set themselves up in the second building. Print media (the radical newspaper *Il Manifesto*,[112] the magazine *Carta*,[113] etc.) took the first floor, Radio GAP[114] occupied the second, and Indymedia the third.

ManO: *I answered the call to lend a hand, so… it was the 16 July… together with other people from Naples I left and went to the school where they were putting together this media center. This was not just an Indymedia escapade – there was that initial core of Indymedia but many other political groups as well. And fundamentally many people that are now in Autistici or other similar projects met there lending a hand building the media center. We moved from knowing each other virtually and through chat to meeting in person; this was important for me, because by meeting, one increases the level of trust from the generic type one can develop online.*

They came together through the Hackmeeting list to build the technical infrastructure that would support the hard work of Indymedia as well as the legal team, laying cables, setting up the servers and workstations…

ManO: *What I fundamentally understood is that we were five years behind in Naples! I felt lost. Also from a technical standpoint, what I was able to do was minimal compared with what the others did, what they'd learned in the hacklabs.*

In fact the level of technology deployed in those days was impressive but, as is often the case, behind the scenes they confronted all sorts of problems.

---

111 Varazze: A small town of 14,000 souls located on the Liguria riviera west of Genoa.
112 *Il Manifesto*: Born from a dissident group of the same name inside the Communist Party, *Il Manifesto* began as a monthly magazine in 1969. It became a daily newspaper in 1971 as its members either were expelled from the Party or drifted away of their own accord. Today it is not formally aligned with any political party.
113 *Carta:* Left-wing Italian magazine.
114 Radio GAP: Collaborative radio station put together by existing free radio projects to cover the events during the G8 in Genoa. Amongst the stations involved were: Radio OndaRossa (Rome); Radio Black Out (Turin); Radio Onda d'Urto (Brescia).

Caparossa: *We were in the Pascoli school, where the media center was, but so many people arrived that there wasn't space for all of them. Then it was decided, before everything started, on the Tuesday or Wednesday before the demonstrations, to cable the Diaz school as well, something that wasn't initially anticipated. So we bought long cables and threw them to the other side of the street, stringing them up in the trees. I have this beautiful memory of some guys who made a lasso like cowboys, twirled it like John Wayne and threw it up into the tree. Then one of them climbed the tree and tossed it again from there into the street and brought it inside the school. A marvelous display. And Diaz was cabled with four, five computers (running Debian of course) that were completely destroyed during the raid on Saturday night.*

At that exact moment the media center, Hackmeeting, and newly born A/I, overlapped with the members working all hours of the day. In fact, A/I and Indymedia were two political projects powered by more or less the same people.

Bomboclat: *We made long-lasting friendships there. Faust, for example, is a Genoese guy I met at the time who later joined Autistici.*

In the media center, some of those in Indymedia subsequently joined A/I, and vice versa; many members of Autistici/Inventati who provided the technical back-up during those days became permanent subscribers to the Indymedia list.

Man0: *One of the people there in Genoa was Blicero. One day he talked to me about the project of Autistici (he talked to me about it after Genoa and not in August, so it must have been September-October), he explained to me how it worked, I felt comfortable with it and told him 'eh why not? Sign me up to the list, within the limits of my abilities I will try to lend a hand'.*

The countersummit took place between the 19 and 22 July 2001. There were marches planned for the three days of Friday, Saturday, and Sunday.

Pinke: *Many people from A/I went a week earlier to help set up the Indymedia media center. I went a few days early, without participating in the preparations taking place on the ground. Anyway in Genoa I slept in the media center, my friends were there. During the day, I divided myself between groups, I went a bit with one, and a bit with others.*

In Genoa, the situation was critical. The city was crawling with cops, violence was predicted and for the final demonstration a hundred times the number of people that normally participate were expected. An uncontrollable situation loomed on the horizon.

As stated the various political communities were very perplexed about if – and how – to join the counter-summit that had been organized for months and months by the Genoa Social Forum.[115] The same tensions were reflected in the commitments taken by some members of A/I who were also involved with Indymedia. Some decided to step back before everything started.

---

115 Genoa Social Forum (GSF): The left reformist component of the protest movement mobilizing against the G8. Its figurehead was Vittorio Agnoletto, subsequently elected as a member of the European Parliament for Communist Refoundation. In the post G8 debate, some members of the GSF (and others) blamed more radical demonstrators for the violence, a position which generated enormous amounts of bad feeling.

Mille: *At that time Indymedia was an extensive milieu with A/I at its core, fifty or so people in total, who set up the media center in Genoa. A few months before the G8, we unexpectedly found ourselves with three hundred and fifty members. I personally noticed there was a high level of tension and a low level of activism. There were those who joined with the best of intentions; those who joined to write a dissertation; those for curiosity's sake; and those to spy. The massive wave of subscriptions came from the expectations placed on the event by the official media. At that point, my instinct was to step back and I went to Genoa simply as a protester. I wrote a long mail to the list to explain my reasons (in which I criticize and self-criticize the project). Stampa clandestina would later publish the whole thing and wheat-paste it all over the city.*

Inventati arrived in Genoa and joined Autistici in the buildings assigned by the city. After the abandonment of various campgrounds due to downpours that left them unusable, the Diaz school became principally a dormitory, while in the Pascoli space was made for the media center, infirmary, and legal service.

Pinke: *I believe that the G8 affected the collective's history. In the most important memories I have of those days, I was almost always with people from the collective. Maybe it's really this experience that united us and created a true collective. From one side, Genoa showed that the philosophical jerking off and paranoia made sense; and from the other, it meant that for all the force we could muster, it wasn't a fair fight. Knowledge and preparation aren't enough against a show of brute force. We lost. What more could have been done except bringing everyone into the streets? We gave everything and achieved nothing.*

On Thursday the migrants' demonstration went smoothly. But as everyone knows, on Friday afternoon the tension rose, there was intense street fighting and Carlo Giuliani[116] died in Piazza Alimonda. In the media center, writing the twenty lines for the day's feature, they knew they had to dot the i's and cross the t's.

Cojote: *It wasn't only our friends and comrades reading Indymedia the next day, but thousands of people. In such a dramatic situation, we needed to remain clear headed.*

On Saturday, exceeding even the worst expectations, the city goes to hell and that night the police assault the Diaz school. Almost the entire collective is in the media center, filming the raid from above. Then the Pascoli school is raided.

Radio GAP, which is streaming its broadcasts from the building to the whole world, announces the arrival of the police and stops its live broadcast at 11:57 pm.

For a series of contributing reasons, Pinke is right, and one can say that the collective only exists as we know it after Genoa. There is a chronological factor: A/I had launched its project at the Hackmeeting in Catania only a few weeks before.

It was also the birth of a strong friendship, that special connection that comes from having shared an especially tragic experience.

---

116 Carlo Giuliani: 24-year-old protester shot dead by police during a confrontation on the streets of Genoa on the second day of the G8 summit in 2001.

Blicero: *Genoa was an event of traumatic communion, the second reason for the internal cohesion of the collective. The collective was welded together first by the joy of doing things and by the projection into the future of the things we're doing, because people responded, because what we do is needed and it worked. Because this thing you're doing is new. Then there's a traumatic event. Everyone facing this incredibly huge thing together. In Genoa, you dealt with aggression from the police, you were part of a pack. It's the same aggression that has made you more cohesive. You have an enemy, however indefinite, one who has it in for you. This makes Genoa an emotionally important moment, something you can't pretend to not have shared.*

Finally there is the public exploit, such exposure that quickly and naturally A/I became established as the movement's server.

Pbm: *The success was resounding, not immediate, but resounding.*

Their presence in the media center had in fact allowed A/I to reach an enormous number of people and publicize the project to innumerable groups involved in political, social, and countercultural activism, both Italian and international.

Blicero: *With Genoa, everyone that passed through the media center and Indymedia knew A/I, and they asked us for lists and email addresses. And it expanded. In the meantime, the events that took place put the movement at the center of the world's attention and there's a boom in participation. The growth of A/I is a process born of many factors which were independent of us. We found ourselves in the right place at the right time, we wanted to do it and invest our energy because we knew there really was a need, because we believed it was important.*

As much as the 'traumatic communion' can bind A/I, the shock for those who saw and lived those days wasn't easily digested and not everyone reacted the same way.

Bomboclat: *Regarding the media center in Genoa, there was extraordinary participation and it doesn't make sense to talk about the flags under which people got involved. For A/I it was a moment in which many people joined, but many people left as well. Many individuals backed away due to the ferocity of the fight...*

On the digital front, Genoa was the most recorded, filmed, and photographed demonstration the movement had ever seen. The trials that followed were fought using these digital materials. In substance the G8 opened 'the era of Indymedia' and with it a completely new political paradigm. Those from A/I that remained in Indymedia continued to offer their own peculiar computer and editorial skills, which were increasingly in demand.

Bomboclat: *With the simultaneous experimentation with streaming radio from home, pirate television stations, and online archives, technical steps like data compression have to be made so that the production of an immense amount of content isn't slowed down or impeded by the era's bandwidth limits. A/I fought its own technical battles that were focused on free software, since it wasn't always easy to convince media activists to use Linux and/or change the formats they were used to working with. A lot of debates took place and a lot of training was provided in collectively run spaces.*

Due to what happened from July 2001 onwards, the collective became widely perceived as the movement's tech support.

Blicero: *We found ourselves at the center of history, but this isn't something you plan in advance… anyone, even in the future, that finds themselves in the same situation, will find themselves there because they are doing things and they are stubborn, for a number of reasons that can't be planned. After Genoa, as A/I we continued to encourage the multiplication of servers. Indivia, Oziosi, and other similar projects were born that are very important to us. In the meantime, we gave technical support and looked after all aspects of the movement's communications channels, from radio stations to pirate TV.*

But despite the creation of other independent servers, the majority of the work fell on A/I.

ManO: *In some way, the political, organizational, and even the technical aspect caused a lot of people to choose Autistici. To tell the truth, not knowing the prospects of Teknusi, I did too – of course I always recommended Autistici's services. Except for those things that Autistici doesn't provide much support for, like streaming, which needs a lot of bandwidth. For this we've raised funds… quite often we resorted to self-financing… we put up a server of our own and used it for streaming.*

And so A/I, a project begun a few months earlier with the idea of following ECN's model, suddenly found itself both witnessing and building the movement's transition from analog to digital.

PART 2: FROM 2001 TO 2006
FROM THE GENOA AFTERMATH
TO THE POLITICS OF EMERGENCY

Setting the Scene, 2001-2006

Whatever way one interpreted it, the G8 in Genoa was a watershed which opened a crisis already present in the movement. After Genoa it was difficult to articulate a common vision, and a phase of dizzying fragmentation began.

Things seemed somehow unreal and people were still unable to clearly comprehend the murder of Carlo Giuliani, the brutality in the Diaz School and Bolzaneto Police Barracks,[117] and the two days of beatings and street fighting with the police. When the televised debates, the accusations and the insults ended, investigations were opened. In February the TPO social center in Bologna, the Cecco Rivolta squat in Florence, the Gabrio social center in Turin, and the headquarters of the Cobas[118] union in Taranto were searched as the supposed headquarters of Indymedia Italy. In reality Indymedia has no headquarters, and only in the TPO all videos were confiscated, to be used to prepare for the trials related to the street clashes. On the other hand, those who witnessed the raid underlined the investigators' interest in the objects on display in the Sexyshock space, which culminated in the confiscation of a vibrator. Different proceedings began to take shape, some against the demonstrators, some against the police. Of all the structures created for the G8, only the Legal Team survived, supported in its action by the network of volunteers Supporto Legale,[119] who continued to follow the trials amidst a slow but inexorable decline in public interest.

The atmosphere of estrangement was exacerbated after the attack on the twin towers of the 11 September, where the feeling that is well described by the phrase 'state of fear', which the movement had already tasted in Genoa, spread over the whole world. The 'politics of the emergency' became the default practice. The state was 'forced' to act in the face of circumstances, and the need for quick decision-making replaced or, better, completed the already weary democratic practices. It became a *modus operandi* applied to everything, from politics to the economy, not that the two are distinguishable anymore.

In November of 2002, the European Social Forum was held. It was the first large meeting of what had been the movement of Genoa 2001. There were a lot of participants, but ultimately

---

117 Bolzaneto Barracks: Barracks of the Flying Squad (Reparto Mobile), a section of the police for use on demonstrations and in football grounds. During the G8 the barracks was at least partially taken over by the GOM (Gruppo Operativo Mobile), the riot squad used to suppress prison revolts. During those three days, about five hundred people were brought to the barracks for identification, then released or moved to jail. Many were tortured in Bolzaneto, including some who had already been severely beaten in the police raid on the Diaz school.
118 COBAS: One of two large grassroots trade unions (alongside the CUB) active in many sectors.
119 Supporto Legale: Organization set up to co-ordinate the legal work and collect evidence relating to the prosecutions after the G8.

it was a leave-taking, even if many may not have realized it. One million people came to march in the streets of Florence and then nothing happened. People started concentrating on daily survival or just dropped out. And so this international protest movement dozed off to sleep.

In response to the 11 September, the US and NATO launched the military campaign Enduring Freedom in Afghanistan to search for Osama Bin Laden – first an ally against the Soviets, then an arch-enemy, a Magneto, a Moriarty for the 21st century. In 2003, there was the second Gulf war, the execution of Saddam Hussein and the forced democratization of Iraq.

The movement attempted to regroup through the protests against the war, but the atmosphere had been poisoned; governments went their own way and didn't listen to anyone except the United States. During 2002-2003, large demonstrations took place all over the world, but their effect was to display the movement's own powerlessness rather than successfully disrupt decisions which had already been taken.

In Italy, the long decade of Berlusconi governments, with a brief Prodi[120] interval, began. The left blew up and exhausted itself in endless criticism against Silvio Berlusconi, personalizing all issues.

In many cities, corporate restructuring in the large factories had left behind a landscape of empty and desolate shells. Many were resuscitated, like defused bombs, through squatting and self-management. But starting in the 90s, building speculators began to count these shells among their own treasures. After 2000, in various cities including Milan, evictions cut the legs out from under many squats and the life of collectives became more and more difficult. The survival of movement-oriented groups was increasingly complex and required a level of reflection on the political climate and an attention to the local situation that consumed all available energy.

Another period of mourning marked and accompanied the fragmentation of this period. In 2003, Dax, a guy from the Orso squat in the Ticinese neighborhood in Milan, was stabbed by two fascists. A black fog descended on the northern capital, which in those years had become a laboratory of right-wing government. The peak of this turn was perhaps in 2006, when during a rally by the extreme right, an unauthorized anti-fascist demonstration supported by various social centers and political groups was called. The march took place but was broken up by police charges and arrests, and resistance in the city collapsed between misunderstandings and exhaustion. It was a fate shared by many Italian cities. Movements went dormant, with rare but important exceptions: in 2005, in the Susa Valley, 30,000 people occupied the building site of the high-speed train in Venaus,[121] tore down the fences surrounding the site and forced the police to retreat. It felt like re-awakening from a long slumber.

---

120 Romano Prodi: Twice prime minister of Italy (1996-1998, 2006-2008) with a center-left coalition of parties, and 10th president of the European Commission.

121 Venaus: Very small mountain village close to the Susa Valley, from where the struggle against the high-speed train sprouted.

Hacktivism, 2001-2006

The commercial explosion of the web determined the way in which people first encountered the internet, something similar to what had happened with cellphones or with technology in general.

During the 90s, an attempt was made to analyze the impact ICT would have on social life and many anticipated an increase in the number of politically critical communities, able to exploit the horizontality that this means of communication seemed to facilitate. But from 2000 onwards, it was apparent that the evolution of the web wouldn't only be driven from below and that the critical dimension wouldn't occupy center stage, but would instead be marginalized and boxed off, just like in the 'real world'. Somehow a trend had inverted – whereas initially movements tried to exploit technology to their own advantage, now it seemed more like a battle not to lose ground in the sphere of communication that the market had started to offer the masses.

For example cryptography spread, but in a completely different way from the cypherpunk ideas that had fueled *Kriptonite* or the early A/I collective. E-commerce firms sanctioned and imposed it, whilst users mostly found the complications involved in cryptographic tools to be tiresome, and were happy to trade their privacy for free services.

Parallel to this transformation, Indymedia Italy descended into crisis, torn apart by internal fights. During and after Genoa 2001, the project boomed – many people were using the site and its mailing lists following the events of the G8. *Aggiornamento 1*, one of the first video accounts about Genoa to be released, was done by Indymedia Italy. It was a montage of footage filmed by activists at the protests: images from the raid at the Diaz school, cops beating people in the streets, and police charges on the waterfront. Genoa was one of the first situations where it was evident that the traditional world of corporate information would soon have to confront the web, the widespread use of digital video cameras (and, a few years later, videophones and smartphones), and the proliferation of sources and channels for information. However, somehow Indymedia was overcome by its own slogan, made flesh in our society of exhibitionists, voyeurs, and media activists: *Become the media.*

The crisis of Indymedia lasted several years, and saw the closure of the national mailing list and a shift to regional lists. Some simply stopped functioning. Today the project still exists and is trying to recover some sense of meaning.

A/I and all the self-managed servers had difficulty facing these breathtaking developments and the entrenchment on the web of players backed by large amounts of capital and driven by a profit logic. The blogging phenomenon was the first sign of change, followed by the very first social networks, in particular Myspace.

These tools accomplished the idea of giving everybody easy access to the internet, but centralized the circulation of content and sensitive user data in a few large businesses. The web started to change, people became accustomed to the constant presence of the internet and slowly began to expose themselves and their own lives online. The statement 'I met this person on the internet' no longer comes across as eccentric or exotic, but normal, just like 'I met them in a bar'.

Noblogs.org, a blogging platform, but without data mining, was A/I's attempt to take advantage of all the good things offered by these technological developments. It was initially conceived to keep together the critical minds orphaned by the crisis of Indymedia.

The street level was hit by setbacks as well. The crisis of squatting in various cities and the creation of new spaces of learning, especially online, meant the end of many hacklabs that weren't able to cope with the generational turnover or were swept away along with the social centers that had hosted them. The labs that survived continued their activities, but perhaps the experimental aspect was stripped away and replaced by routine. These years were characterized by a sort of strategic retreat into the social centers. The Resistance was frequently talked of; the sensation of abandoning the cities for the mountains and waiting until the end of winter prevailed.

But even if the low level of struggle was obvious, not everything had been pacified. In 2006, the Hackmeeting community produced a small pearl of self-management. They occupied a building in Parma, hooked up water, power, and internet and celebrated their annual and cathartic meeting of nerds and kindred spirits. Perhaps spring was right around the corner…

After Genoa 2001

Void: *Italy was in turmoil in the months immediately after the G8 summit. A lot of people got involved in politics and active in self-managed social centers. What that meant for A/I was an increased number of users. But for our part we continued on as before – discussing issues on the collective's mailing list and tinkering with the servers.*

During these months A/I focused on optimizing its services and resources. In particular the security of the server became a more urgent topic of discussion. The situation after Genoa 2001 was marked by ominous episodes.

Void: *The first security issues arose as soon as we presented the project to the public at the* Hackmeeting. *That's when we did a first redesign of the server box, modifying its initial configuration. After Genoa in 2001, the server was transformed from being a space for our experimentation as hackers into a serious resource.*

However, the shift that caused A/I's activity to cease to be perceived as harmless was not immediate, and the response of the authorities to the various forms of media activism was not uniform.

Cojote: *The first big demonstration after Genoa was the Perugia-Assisi Peace March,[122] which was understandably well attended that year. I drove there in a rented van which we had decorated with Indymedia's black flags. We went there to distribute the first VHS tapes of footage from the anti-G8 protests, which had been edited and supplemented with updated material.*

After the Peace March, the guys parked their camper van in a square in Perugia for two days, setting up a makeshift info-point. Caught unawares, the local authorities supported the initiative and granted it permission.

---

122 Perugia-Assisi Peace March: Annual peace march held in the home city of Saint Francis, who also happens to be the patron saint of Italy.

Cojote: *We had a strange appeal. When a connection was set up between Blicero in Palestine and one of the main squares in Florence, Piazza della Signoria, technicians working for the city offered us the infrastructure, provided a link for the stream and allowed us to erect an antenna. On that occasion we had set up our info-point in the middle of the square without any authorization, but no one tried to kick us out. Today this would be unthinkable. And yet there we were, black-clad… and with attitudes that were anything but social-democratic.*

In the collective's eyes, the tolerance shown by the various city officers towards these initiatives was explicable by the fact that they could not immediately be pigeon-holed. They were a novelty and behaved in ways other than usually expected of the opposition. Long accustomed to a traditional style of political antagonism – and its accompanying grammar of actions, language and demands – local politicians found nothing objectionable about these young 'reporters'.

Cojote: *Media activists tried to be impartial figures. We stood next to journalists and our relationship with authorities was not tainted by the burden of history. It was easy to understand which side we were on, so much so that the help we received on such occasions usually came from insiders, who as individuals decided to give us a hand. But the problem which weighed upon us was the risk of the seizure of our materials by the police, an issue we would have to face shortly after Genoa.*

Indeed they did not have to wait long. In February 2002 the police searched a series of spaces designated as Indymedia's 'headquarters' and seized a range of material: VHS cassettes, computers, and archives related to the G8 in Genoa. In fact, Indymedia never had a headquarters, being an independent online network based on public mailing lists. The physical places targeted in these searches were the office of the Cobas in Taranto (a rank-and-file trades union), the social centers Gabrio in Turin and TPO in Bologna, and the Cecco Rivolta squat in Florence.

In light of these events, it was time for the collective to reflect on what had happened.

Cojote: *After the Indymedia seizures, we began to try and make the data more secure. Back then we were too paranoid, much more than now. That's why A/I is a closed collective and accepts new members only by 'co-optation' – because in that period we were afraid of being infiltrated.*

There are multiple reasons behind this co-optation mechanism, not least the fact that A/I handles sensitive data for half the political movement in Italy. And then there is also the need to keep the resources functioning even in circumstances where there may be internal quarrels.

Ale: *A/I felt the need to organize itself in such a way as to allow trust to be totally transitive, because we are responsible for others' mailboxes, for their data. That's why it's always been a closed collective. A/I survives and evolves by turning to (or 'co-opting') individuals who feel they have the right skills and motivations. In practice, this means that new members are sought and found within those milieus where A/I is already present. These are people who from time to time have had both the will and strength to contribute to the community through this specific project. So what we call 'co-optation' is an informal mechanism that evolves naturally from the shape of our political activity.*

With time, the closed nature of A/I turned out to be a strategic advantage for the survival of the project.

Void: *After Genoa 2001, Autistici remained fairly united, while we watched other projects run into problems. This was also because while we do our own thing in our own separate collectives, within A/I there is a different and more personal type of commitment.*

Co-optation was not the collective's only inbuilt defense mechanism: there was also a sort of 'compartmentalization' born of a shared determination to build something that can endure.

Blicero: *If A/I as a group do not have a shared feeling with regard to a specific question then this matter is automatically excluded from the collective's bailiwick, because the project is more important than any single issue. Within the collective there are people with different political ideas, but that's less important than A/I so an effort is made. However this effort is not made equally by all, the result is sometimes that the most uncompromising positions win out, which can result in sacrificing innovation – and the experimental urge – but this happens so that the collective protects itself.*

Things were constantly changing – which makes them a bit jumbled – not only regarding the relationship with the authorities, but also within the movement, which tried to re-organize after the Genoese massacre. While many people dropped out of political activism, those who remained felt an obligation to keep things functioning. Tensions arising in the relationships between political organizations, whether fertile or sterile in effect, made A/I's existence complex at a local level. For example, Inventati (the Florentine branch of A/I), with its insistence on independence and taking a particular approach to communications work, found itself in a position that was both odd and difficult to handle.

Cojote: *The tolerance shown occasionally by the authorities towards us led to conflicts with the movement, which viewed it as evidence of incoherence on our part. But we never regarded any authority as 'better' because they let us set up an aerial rather than driving us off.*

As we have seen, older activists always looked at counter-information – what we now call media activism – with some mistrust, and Inventati found a true community of support only among the young libertarians of the Cecco Rivolta squat. And even then it was not without difficulties.

Cojote: *We were clearly doing something delicate. In a way we were exposed, the authorities could pick us out easily, and in Florence we were accused or charged with all sorts of things – including unauthorized possession of explosives. On the other hand, we were in direct contact with different parts of the local movement who often refused to speak to one another. In the end they had to trust us, but we also had to be very careful when talking to them.*

It is undeniable that Indymedia managed to do things that a few years before would have been unthinkable. Reports were produced on a wide range of locations and situations – local, national, or international – that the movement had always wanted to make widely known beyond the domain of the alternative media.

Caparossa: *In 2002 there was the Solidarity Caravan in Palestine. Radio OndaRossa and Indymedia organized live broadcasts from over there. Press agencies like Adnkronos stole our reports without quoting the source because they had no journalists willing to risk being shot by Israeli troops in the media center in Jenin. It's not that we were cool: we were just* *there. Because we could be there. Because we had the relationships, the contacts. Because we had created a universe of physical and digital communication that enabled us to be on the spot in those years.*

Once again everything is done with affordable equipment: a video camera costing a few hundred euro, a cheap stills camera, a laptop, and a shaky connection.

Caparossa: *The tools were just means to an end, they were not our main focus. Going to Jenin to create a media center was not something for nerds: it was a political action in the most positive and beautiful sense, because we were giving those people the possibility of communicating with the rest of the world – a possibility which otherwise they never would have had.*

European Social Forum

The next stop for the movement was the European Social Forum, held in November 2002 in Florence. Many of those present presumed there would be a media center run by Indymedia like in Genoa, but at this point Indymedia was completely in crisis.

Blicero: *During preparations for the Social Forum in Florence, the fight within Indymedia goes nuclear. It's a moment of strategic choices that are experienced differently. From then on the strong sense of community that there had been between media activists, hackers, and all those active in the movement falls apart. The trust between people collapses and the decline begins.*

Indymedia grew a lot after Genoa, constantly earning more credibility. But with so much visibility came an inevitable change that ended up altering the relationships between media activists.

Bomboclat: *Since the beginning the main fight was whether Indymedia should be considered a political group and how its influence was to be managed. This and other questions transform Indymedia Italy into a mirror of the different positions within the movement. But it's really about social or political pressure. What's really corrosive is the way people relate to each other within the project – a pattern that will alienate them from one another. A familiar process is triggered, typical of informal groups, and if it's not acknowledged or discussed, and the problems are not tackled immediately, it ends up tearing the group apart.*

For its part, the A/I collective did not participate in the ESF in any organized fashion. Some of them decided to work at Hub, others at the ESF media center.

Caparossa: *For the organization of the Social Forum in Florence, I had Blicero's role, how lucky for me... Blicero had decided to do something else, and the Hub is born from that decision. There was a terrible fight because out of the blue Gradozero and him decided to do the Hub.*

They decided that the media center experience had been done and it was necessary to go beyond it. They said it was necessary to do something more advanced, autonomous from the organization of the Social Forum, to characterize ourselves in a different way, and that they would only enter the ESF to protest it.

Some committed to managing the technical aspects of the various structures of the Social Forum as paid work.

Mille: *It was business. The ESF preferred somebody local and they called Inventati as we were well known in Florence, but if they hadn't entrusted the job to us, it would have gone to a private company. I myself went to the preparatory meetings and each time they said, 'Indymedia will do the media center', I intervened to correct them, although I understand that when the same people are involved it can be difficult to distinguish between the acronyms. At the time we wore different 'hats' depending on what we were doing.*

Others left Florence or attended the events as spectators.

Pinke: *I wouldn't participate in the Social Forum because I saw it as a meaningless, ostentatious, media event. I didn't want to be there with so-called 'pacifists' in the period after Genoa, of legal fights and pro and anti-Black Bloc divisions... to be polite, I couldn't stand them. There was a large debate inside Indymedia and to some degree in A/I. I remember Blicero as the one who pushed us to get involved with the Hub, but I said no. During a large Indymedia meeting I stated my disagreement with participating in the ESF, as did the rest of Indymedia Tuscany.*

During the ESF, Ale, who later became responsible for a number of ideas and important insights, came into contact with the collective.

Blicero: *The Social Forum in Florence is very important because we got Ale involved in the existence of A/I. At the ESF Ale meets Bombo and C1cc10, and they rope him into Autistici. His involvement doesn't begin immediately, it takes almost a year, but his contribution will then be fundamental from both a technical point of view and beyond...*

Let's not forget that during the time of the ESF, A/I is discussing internally how to improve the security of the machine in case of a possible seizure. Unfortunately at the same time Pbm, the server guru, Mr-Wolf-I-Solve-Problems, the technical expert, was stepping back and couldn't be asked to do much more than sustain the structure as it was.

Pbm: *I always managed the server during the first three years. But after that, for personal reasons and due to work, I gradually had less and less time to devote to the project, as soon as possible I stepped aside because I couldn't do it any more. But in the months leading up to that, I was increasingly detached. During the fall of 2004, I almost never touched the server.*

When Cojote brought up the problems of the collective with him, Ale proposed a number of technical solutions. They started to outline what three years later became known as Plan R*.

Pbm: *Until the launch of Plan R* I really felt responsible for the server, also because my technical skills were broader. I was the only person who could do everything at the same time. Fortunately, in the meantime, other people arrived that really wanted to do it and moreover were technically very competent. They gradually took over what I did... and I took the opportunity to distance myself from A/I.*

So began the ceaseless transformation which led to the change of the technical structure of A/I in a few short years. But the ESF was a decisive juncture also for other reasons. Indymedia reorganized itself after an explosive internal conflict, but inside the management list the level of internal agreement continued to decline.

Blicero: *During the political ebb that followed the ESF, A/I is saved by its smaller size. There were given limits to what it did and didn't do. Indymedia was too open and public, it couldn't limit itself and on the other hand couldn't go on as it was because it had become unmanageable, it needed organization. In practice, however, it doesn't survive the change.*

Also Inventati, after this experience, didn't have many other alternatives than retreat. The tensions disrupted their milieu and after the ESF, the Florentines found themselves picking up the bill for the fallout from the explosive dynamics that had been triggered.

Caparossa: *The ebb would have been the same. But in Florence it was like a bomb went off. In Florence everything vanished. Everyone huddled around what little was left standing. And for the little that remained, the evictions began, the charges rained down, it was a massacre. A political and human massacre, because people stopped talking to each other, even people within A/I.*

Kaos Tour and Communications Strategies

A/I's economic situation was extremely unstable (perhaps non-existent would be more accurate). The collective was financed through the political groups to which its members belonged and a few subscriptions.

Alieno: *For the Bologna Hackmeeting in 2002, we made t-shirts and sweatshirts with the legend '+kaos' to finance the project. Everybody wanted one and it helped to create a collective imagination we carry with us to this day.*

The lack of funding inspired a series of ingenious solutions such as when, in July of 2002, the server Paranoia irreparably broke. While Bomboclat and C1cc10 were at work, a co-worker of theirs, sympathetic to A/I's misfortune, put a 3D rendering computer at their disposal, replacing the machine and saving the data. The two autistics, a PC under their arm, hopped on a tram and ran to fix the situation.

Bomboclat: *The new server took the name Chernobyl by virtue of its odd dual processor. However, that computer was lent to us, and in turn was replaced with Astio, named after our grudge (astio) against this unhappy world. The collective suffered constant pressure and the police department responsible for monitoring communications had already visited the office where the server was hosted a few times.*

Astio was assembled at LOA, this time not from recycled hardware, but following a DIY approach.

Pbm: *We liked the idea of a 'DIY server', which was also a way of getting the best and simultaneously saving some money. The results weren't exactly great. We made mistakes during assembly, chose components that weren't fully compatible with each other. There was no end to the problems that server gave us, until ultimately we had to replace it.*

Meanwhile, this was a difficult period for the Milanese hacklab. The Bulk was under threat of eviction and at a certain point the electricity was cut off. They decided to continue courses as planned with the aid of a noisy generator, but the situation was clearly unsustainable. As the space hosting it emptied, LOA become progressively more dormant, and without a physical point of reference people began to drift off.

Some people remained in touch, while others joined A/I. Bomboclat, C1cc10, and Blicero continued their involvement, setting up computer networks in social centers in exchange for hosting their projects aimed at promoting free software. For a while the Milanese were forced into a nomadic existence.

Bomboclat: *We organized nights during which we played and talked. The* sniffer*-parties were memorable, with internet-connected computers hooked up to a projector, to illustrate case by case to activists where they had screwed up in terms of privacy protection and how not to leave any* logs.

But LOA's closure was the result of larger issues, not just the electricity being cut off. In the same period, many of the other hacklabs that had sprouted up throughout Italy during 2000 either closed their doors or went into hibernation. In the case of Italy the change had begun in July 2001, after which nothing would ever be the same.

The political paradigm was being redefined for everyone when in 2003 some refugees from LOA launched ReLOAd, an internet café inside the space Pergola.

The people who took part in this activist experience inside a non-squatted space (which made it somewhat controversial in those days) felt part of a continuum, given that their reflection on the political possibilities hadn't stopped and ReLOAd was the result.

Bomboclat: *We made the move together from nerdism to* Serpica Naro, *always on the front lines, always ready to respond to needs as soon as they emerged. The ability to change was our strength.*

After the closure of LOA, the political downturn and a series of other unfortunate circumstances, the end of free hosting for the server approached inexorably.

Given the bandwidth it consumed, there weren't many other solutions except turning to a commercial provider.

Pbm: *After a long troubled period at my workplace, I changed jobs. I went to work with a large manufacturer and couldn't bring the server with me.*

By 2003, A/I hosted 205 sites, 2046 users, and 269 discussion lists. Things had gone too far to think about closing up shop. No matter how cheap, the estimate for decent hosting was thousands of euros a year. To pay for it out of their own pockets was unfeasible. It was necessary to take a different route: a fundraising campaign. That's how the KAOS tours were born.

Bomboclat: *It's not only an economic question. Living on the internet, the collective is a completely de-territorialized political project. To keep the members updated and, especially,* convince them to use properly the tools provided to them, the newsletter isn't always sufficient. In order to share technological innovations with the movement and communicate new ideas requiring explanation, it's necessary to go and meet people.

On the 14 and 15 March, the Roman event for the first KAOS Tour was held in the squatted space Strike. With the help of many kindred collectives (like Candida TV), they filled a thick program with activities and actions. Everyone contributed their time and skills.

Bomboclat: *For three days we did workshops on how to configure a server, use encryption, create a visual archive, stream audio, edit video and put it online.*

In tandem with this, Strike organized workshops on the Italian computer community, the GNU-economy, digital rights and hacker ethics (thanks to the support of the guys from BUGS Lab; they also got 'cabled' in thanks for their hospitality). Lectures were also given on the radio and at La Sapienza University of Rome. There were thematic theater performances, music and DJ sets at night.

Pinke: *The first KAOS Tour was really beautiful, it was the first thing we did together after Genoa, and meeting our users was marvelous because... we liked them! The KAOS Tour helped us realize that A/I was building a community. Not only making tools, not just being a provider. During the KAOS Tour it became clear that people felt deeply involved in the whole process. This community has grown over the years, step by step, but here it is. It's a community that goes beyond the people who form the collective.*

Another valuable aspect was that it was a chance for the members of the collective to meet not only each other, but also many other hackers who had built and participated in the Italian scene over the previous years.

Mille: *There was an amazing discussion at Strike. In the same room there was us from A/I, ECN, Strano Network, part of the Florence hacklab, some people from TMCrew and people who had worked on the BBS networks like AvANa... fifteen years of Italian online projects in a room having a freewheeling conversation.*

The KAOS Tour in Rome was a moment of sharing and self-education for the movement. Although Autistici/Inventati was ostensibly the subject under discussion, the goal was really the presentation of tools, services, and a lot of other projects.

Void: *In Bologna we had set up inside the TPO social center. We had a computer lab there, and thanks to the center's economic resources it was really well equipped, especially for video. Not everyone liked it, but it was an independent space, a reference point used by a lot of different people: students, activists, but also people who just needed advice on how to configure a computer. So we became well known in Bologna, mainly through face to face interactions, like Inventati in Florence. However, on the A/I list the common need for a roadshow for the project emerged.*

With the proceeds of the first KAOS Tour, A/I set up the server in Aruba's web farm in Arezzo, south west of Florence.

After the first event at Strike, others followed both large and small. The model for KAOS Tour was actually a traveling circus – a form of presentation that combined the key experiences of the hacklabs, the Hackmeeting universe, and the Milanese evenings inaugurated during the first years of ECN.

Void: *We started as always from what ECN had done, that is going to social centers and sparking a debate. The difference was that at the time of ECN nobody knew what the internet was, whereas now people not only know what it is, but it's common to have an email address or use the web. So we decided to organize events all over Italy in the places that had similar politics to ours. The events reflect in part the spirit of the Hackmeetings: moments of sociality on one hand, and workshops on the other.*

From that year on, the KAOS Tour label encompassed all events aimed at raising funds, debates, alternative media, and the presentation of the project organized by A/I in local areas.

Void: *The first KAOS Tour in Bologna takes place in 2005 in the Crash! social center, where there had already been seminars and introductory courses for the internet in 2004, but without either parties or a name.*

2005 was also the most demanding year because of the repression that led to the Aruba crackdown. After this the collective felt itself obliged to tour and explain the disaster that had taken place. We'll see later what happened there. Compared with a newsletter and other digital communications, however, the KAOS Tour in 2003 was an immense communications exploit by A/I, a collective effort shared with various political groups.

Alieno: *At the beginning, the KAOS Tour was a way to talk to the community and say, 'look, all of this is a political approach to computers, the people who do this aren't angels on the internet, but people who are thinking about the world with you'. Because of this, the spaces that hosted us did the graphics for the events, only in 2005 do we go to the trouble of printing a single poster for all the dates and this will be with a design made for us by Blu.*

In 2003, the collective still had a rough communications strategy. All communications efforts took place on the site, as is logical, where particularly the Inventati part had been redesigned several times over the years, always for strategic reasons.

Alieno: *At the time the web presence was split between the group from LOA who had made the home page of autistici.org and the Florentines who kept changing inventati.org in search of a version that would work. For example, on the first home page (in blue and black!) there was no space for news, but the red and black re-design of 2003 has space for news updates too.*

In any event, things changed in 2004. The collective was forced to confront the communication question and not only to deliver technical warnings to its community.

Alieno: *We had our first real communications emergency in 2004, around the Trenitalia case. Then there was a decent level of production of materials. We circulated DIY booklets where we described what happened. We who were involved needed to keep public attention on what was happening. Trenitalia was the first major incident. After this experience, the necessity to have a good balance between news and graphics appears. Thanks to Shah and Echomrg, who have some experience with this, the unified home page appears in the second half of the year.*

Legal Cases – Trenitalia, 2004

The Facts

In July 2004, the Investici Association received a subpoena from the train operator, Trenitalia. They were accused of hosting a web page that imitated the design of Trenitalia's site. Following the almost classic practice of *détournement*, the page mocked the train company and denounced their role in support of the second Gulf war.

During the maneuvers leading up to the war (March 2003), Italian trains were used to move tanks and war supplies to and from the numerous American bases present in the peninsula. This news provoked great controversy and protests.

The site – which still exists, at *autistici.org/zenmai23/trenitalia* – was conceived by a collective of designers that had already disbanded at the time of the subpoena.

Trenitalia made multiple demands including immediate deletion of a page that was 'horribly offensive to the company'; published notification of its removal in two newspapers (*Corriere della Sera*, the Italian equivalent of *The New York Times*, and *Sole 24ore*, the country's leading business press, at a cost of 'only' 20,000 euros); the elimination of metatags referring to Trenitalia; and compensation for 'moral and material damages'.

After a series of hearings to decide on the urgency of the court order, the collective was notified that it was obliged to comply immediately with the demand.

A/I was forced to take down the cheeky site, but also appealed against the decision.

Unfortunately for Trenitalia, the attempt at censorship ensured that the offending web page was reproduced on mirror sites all over the web.

In August, Italy fell into a sweaty lethargy and didn't return to normal until September.

At the appeal hearing of the 7 September, Trenitalia relaunched their case asking for 'the extension of the injunction to every page with the same content'.

In practice, Trenitalia asked A/I to also remove the list of those mirrors that had appeared spontaneously on the internet. This was judicially controversial, because if it was a crime to link to something on the internet, then any search engine could be considered criminal.

Once again a description of the internet that had nothing to do with the law was advanced in a court. Trenitalia's lawyers benefited from the lack of a widespread understanding of digital culture to argue a case which was baseless but did raise a number of difficult issues. For example, to what extent should a hypothetical service provider, also a commercial host, be considered responsible for the content on its machines? In the brief filed with the court, they attributed authorship of the site to the Investici Association – confusing 'domain' with 'site'.

Lawyers for the collective presented a press dossier containing a collection of news stories about Trenitalia. The contents focused on known facts regarding Trenitalia. The collection didn't so much deal with those who had come out in support of Investici as to highlight

Trenitalia's troubled role as 'the army's stooge' – stories about protests, layoffs, and other complaints. The Trenitalia case was followed with great interest both on and off the net. The use of the courts against an obvious case of satire angered a lot of people. Many added their voice in support of A/I. On the 14 September, the court granted A/I's appeal and the site was put back online. Meanwhile Trenitalia was obliged to pay the legal costs.

The Verdict

The verdict confirmed that the defendant's site constituted satire, an activity whose legitimacy 'is recognized and protected by the law as a particular expression of the freedom of thought and criticism and is therefore encompassed by the scope of protection guaranteed by article 21 (of the Constitution)'.

The court also recognized that the satire hadn't crossed the line into 'gratuitous insult', because it really 'had a reliable basis in fact within the dialectic and actual elements that gave rise to the controversy'.

In essence, 'the assistance provided to Italian participation in war operations in Iraq' was well known at the time, as was the fact that Trenitalia had been heavily criticized by the peace movement and 'that numerous protests were called due to such transports'.

The verdict, stunning everyone, closed by responding to the concerns implicit in the entire debate – the abuse of copyright, an umbrella question relevant to many similar situations.

> On the level of copyright protection – this area wasn't dealt with in this preliminary injunction[123] hearing, but is where one finds the most important studies on this point and is thus relevant for purposes of giving a general account of the protection possible under the legal codes – it is generally agreed that works of parody are of their nature independent works, since they anyhow imply creative activity (however modest), and must therefore be protected according to articles 1 and 2 of the copyright law, since they have their own independent originality.[124]

The matter was thus concluded – gloriously, even if for a while it was feared that Trenitalia might want to go to a full trial. On the other hand the Investici Association could have claimed damages.

Fortunately, the train company gave up and the collective could return to its daily chores. Unfortunately at the same time something else was taking place at Aruba's web farm, something that would shake the very roots of A/I's work.

---

123 Preliminary injunction: An order made by a court in a case prior to a full hearing on the merits. Theoretically it should be granted where failure to do so would result in irreparable damage to the plaintiff. Notionally the grant of such an order should not have any bearing on the outcome should the case come to trial.

124 Court of Milan, appeal verdict on Associazione Investici vs. Trenitalia SpA case, https://www.autistici.org/ai/trenitalia/documenti/5_sentenza_ricorso.

Towards Plan R* A/I's Inadvertent Centrality

A/I's work mostly comprised maintaining its internet services. Then in 2005 came the shock of the Aruba case – a wake-up call for the collective and everyone in the community.

However, since there were no serious legal consequences, the episode can be seen as an overdue lesson that forced a confrontation with reality. It was a decisive moment where it was decided that this type of disaster could never happen again.

Pinke: *Aruba was another moment in our evolution because we realized it was wrong to hypothesize levels of security that we couldn't guarantee.*

Although Italy had other self-managed servers, A/I had involuntarily become central to the provision of tech services for the movement. Even if the collective believed that the solution was in a generalization of such servers rather than a centralization around them.

Ale: *Let's take Indivia, set up by people from Bologna connected to the social center XM24. At its roots, there's an interesting proposal to operate servers out of private homes… but although they can effectively host mailboxes and sites, they have to limit themselves to a certain type of local use because they lack the necessary structure to deal with the trials and lawsuits that inevitably accompany any expansion.*

Beyond the strictly legal questions, with time it became clear that the plan to spread independent servers wasn't succeeding for both organizational and technical reasons. Paradoxically, this was also because there was a concentration of users on A/I.

ManO: *During the early years, Autistici advocated the multiplication of self-managed servers. Teknusi was born as a sort of testbed and hosted lists and mailboxes. But in a choice between Teknusi and Autistici, many people chose Autistici. Some had a backup mailbox for times when Autistici went down, which can happen. If a server gets confiscated or something doesn't work, there's an automatic backup on Teknusi and they're going to use the list there as well.*

Through communications to their users, the collective tried to push the distribution of content toward other servers – Indivia, Oziosi, Teknusi, ECN… The aim was to prevent A/I from turning into a major target as the movement's service provider. But it was a damage limitation policy more than a real strategy. It wasn't realistic to just hope that providers would multiply magically in the coming months, so it had already been decided to execute a plan for decentralization internally.

Bomboclat: *Aruba had taught us that you can't trust anybody in Italy, so Autistici's data is now all over the world. To not respond at a technical level would have meant collaborating politically, albeit indirectly, with a wave of repression involving our users in long and absurd court cases.*

Plan R*, therefore, was the collective's answer to a long reactionary period which wasn't limited to the repression of political activists but was devouring the whole society. The Aruba case, with all of its actual and potential implications, was merely the straw that broke the camel's back.

Pbm: *Aruba was the breaking point. Ale had already carried out a study of how to replicate and distribute data, because the number of users was constantly increasing. A/I's original structure was by then inadequate, and the collective was already thinking about what to do in case of a server breakdown. The Aruba case was instrumental in putting that study into practice.*

Legal Cases – Aruba Crackdown, 2004-2005

The Anarchist Black Cross and the Arrests of May 2005

Everything began at the end of May 2005, on the 25 to be exact, when the president of the Investici Association received an order for the removal of the email account croceneraanarchica@inventati.org – the Italian Anarchist Black Cross's mailbox.

The lawyers were consulted but nothing could be done to oppose it, so the demand was passed on to the techs of the collective. They were forced to perform what they regarded as an act of censorship.

A/I often received demands by fax and telephone calls from the DIGOS,[125] but when faced with an order from a court they had to yield and delete the account. Besides the email account on inventati.org, the police also 'pre-emptively' seized several Hotmail accounts and the web page of the Anarchist Black Cross. The preemptive seizure, unusual enough on its own, had been decided a few days before by the Court of Rome with the active collaboration of the Prosecutor of Bologna. This took place in the context of an investigation that led to arrests and searches throughout Italy on the morning of the 26 May.

The warrant talked of 'connections between supporters of individual affinity groups' and argued that 'the communications between the various groups occurred principally through a website and an email account'.

The individual charges were extremely serious and based on articles 270 and 270-bis of the Criminal Code, with indictments for bombings, arms offenses, and anarcho-insurrectionist conspiracy with the aim of terror and subversion (!). The prosecution was based on supposedly 'serious evidence of guilt', because the messages from the Hotmail account – also registered to the Anarchist Black Cross – showed 'the passage of association members from simple ideological adhesion to the level of action'.

This was a totally new situation for Autistici/Inventati. There had been requests for personal data or the log of a certain user before, but the collective couldn't provide the information because it wasn't recorded by the servers. All that was just business as usual.

But the preemptive seizure and closure of an account was an oddity in terms of dealings with law enforcement.

---

125 Divisione Investigazioni Generali Operazioni Speciali (DIGOS): General Investigation and Special
     Operation Division. Branch of the Italian police charged with investigating and acquiring intelligence
     on political and social activities which may result in crimes, and more specifically those suspected to
     be somewhat subversive of democracy. It mostly investigates cases involving domestic terrorism and
     organized crime. It is popularly regarded as the Italian political police.

From a long-term point of view, this crackdown on activists' digital activities had precedents in the Cosenza arrests of 2002[126] and the seizure of Indymedia's server in 2004,[127] and marked another step on the Italian state's path towards greater censorship and control.

It was also a moment in which the disproportionate number of telephone taps made Italian citizens the most 'spied' upon in Europe. The state expenditure for this giant panopticon was already under the eyes of the critical Italian press, with a cost hovering around 300 million euros a year – and talk of 140,000 tapped cellular phones in 2004 at Telecom Italia alone.

It was the time of the articles on Enigma, the electronic brain based at Campobasso that rendered obsolete the classic spies who tapped and listened to individual phone calls, replacing them with a digital system for recording and storing data. Obviously it had become common practice to monitor the private activity of citizens on the internet without losing much sleep over it.

The digital revolution made social control even more pervasive – the more communication is fragmented into many different forms, the more it becomes possible to watch people's private lives. With cellphones becoming indispensable, 'friendly' security cameras everywhere, and with the complicity of commercial service providers facilitating access to the electronic correspondence of citizens, the work of the police had never been easier.

Following the events of the 26 May, Autistici/Inventati released a stern statement together with Isole nelle Rete, which hosted the Anarchist Black Cross's site. However unpleasant this had been, it was ironically only the tip of the iceberg.

Courtesy Visits to Aruba 1.0

Let's take a step back. In 2003, the first KAOS tour was aimed at financing the hosting for A/I's server, given that it was no longer possible to have it hosted for free by a friend. The outcome of this campaign was the movement of the server to Aruba, one of the least costly providers at the time. As it would later come out, on the 15 June 2004, a unit of the branch of the police responsible for monitoring communications, on orders from the Prosecutor of Bologna, paid a courtesy visit to the Arezzo company demanding access to Autistici/Inventati's server. Under pressure, of course, Aruba's technicians switched off the machine and let the agents copy whatever files they wanted from the disk, and, it's thought, perhaps, install a sniffer.

Meanwhile, when the collective asked for an explanation of their server's downtime, Aruba's answer was that there had been 'a technical fault with the cabinet's electrical outlet'. This raid

---

126 Cosenza arrests of 2002: Twenty people were arrested for alleged terrorism in connection with the protests and clashes of the previous year in Naples and Genoa. The warrants were issued by the Court of Justice of Cosenza, Calabria. Among the arrested was Francesco Caruso, a young student and public figure considered one of the leaders of the movement in the south, who was taken to the maximum security prison of Trani.

127 Indymedia server seizure 2004: In October 2004 servers hosting Indymedia sites in Italy and Switzerland were seized by the FBI. Incredibly the computers involved were located in London, although property of a US company, Rackspace, and the FBI explained the seizure as being based on a request by Swiss and Italian criminal investigators. The transnational seizure was enabled by a Mutual Legal Assistance Treaty request which is designed to enable cross-border criminal inquiries.

would be subsequently justified by the investigators by the need to intercept the messages of a single mailbox, the very same the police ordered the collective to cancel on the 26 May of the following year, namely croceneraanarchica@inventati.org.

But what makes this even more grotesque is they compromised the confidentiality of the other 30,000 users.

That Awful Mess on the Via Sergio Ramelli, Fascist Martyr

Let's go back to 2005 and the official request for the cancellation of the email address.

After having deleted the Anarchist Black Cross's mailbox, the Investici Association – as an interested party – in turn solicited the Prosecutor of Bologna (in charge of the investigation) for copies of the procedural documents.

Within the documents was a general report by the Raggruppamento Operativo Speciale (ROS, the main investigative arm of the Carabinieri which deals with organized crime and terrorism) on what was described as the Italian insurrectionist anarchist scene, and a report by the anti-terrorism police on the relevant investigation, that had led to the seizure, arrests and raids of that May.

The investigation turned out to be the same that, with the pretext of acquiring one user's logs, had allowed the FBI to seize the server hosting Indymedia Italy in October of 2004 (alas that Indymedia's server didn't record any logs either).

Reading the procedural documents, some members of the collective noticed that the emails that appeared as evidence were not only those from the Hotmail address, whose interception was mentioned in the warrant, but also some from the Inventati email address, the same they had closed following the interception of messages on Hotmail.

Something didn't add up. The emails in the documents couldn't possibly be in the investigators' hands through legal means, nor have come from an email address that had already been shut down.

The police must have had access to Autistici/Inventati's server.

A more careful reading of the DIGOS's reconstruction, or more precisely, of a footnote, turned out to reveal that to decode the communications of the person suspected of being the sender of various newsletters, it had been necessary to go to Aruba, access the server and take the SSL certificates. And this had taken place on the 15 June of the previous year.

Needless to say, Aruba could have resisted this 'acquisition of documents' because they were in no way legally responsible for the server, which was the property of the Investici Association.

So, almost by chance, the gravity of the events of the Aruba affair came to light.

By the 21 June 2005, the server traffic had likely been compromised for a year and files had been intercepted by police staff without authorization by the courts.

The method used to accomplish the tap entailed a complete violation of the fundamental liberties for everyone using A/I.

It was an abuse worthy of the best dystopias, as the collective wrote in one of the many statements that followed.

Parliamentary Inquiries

On the 12 July, a question on the abuse of the users of the Investici Association was heard before the European Parliament. The instigator of the question, Vittorio Agnoletto, briefly summarized what had happened:

> Without informing the responsible parties at Investici, Aruba's technicians allowed their servers to be shut down and police agents to recover information and sensitive data about a significant number of users. The owners of Investici were kept in the dark about these facts until the 26 May 2005, when they discovered almost accidentally the abuse they were victims of, that had allowed the Italian police forces to have indiscriminate and unauthorized access to sensitive data and to the correspondence of all users (almost 5,000 mailboxes and more than 30,000 in the discussion lists).[128]

On the 22 July, a parliamentary question in Italy by the Green Party Deputies Mauro Bulgarelli and Paolo Cento concluded by asking for an investigation into Aruba and their atrocious practice of not respecting privacy laws and freedom of expression. In a moment when everyone was already talking about the fact that the tapping of telephone calls was out of control, a new and absurd situation loomed for people using the internet too. On one hand, commercial providers like Hotmail had no issue with providing the police forces with their customers' data, without informing them. On the other, as the outraged communication of the collective stated, even trusting people committed to their users' privacy wasn't a solution – 'we can't know what nor how much information law enforcement can take from our and your sites or servers; we can't know for what use they'll put it to nor for how long; we can't know if the providers reserve the same treatment for the requests of their generous competitors or marketing agencies for personal data.'

To confirm the sense of siege this episode provoked in the computer community, during the same days the 'main server' of the Firenze Linux User Group (FLUG) was also compromised.

To give an offhand sense of the damage, it's worth mentioning the information contained in only one of the accounts published at the time on Indymedia. The violation of Autistici/ Inventati's server had directly affected the Genoa Legal Forum; the lawyers' mailboxes, those of their technical consultants and the coordination mailing list were in fact all hosted on a server for which the police held the cryptographic key.

---

128 Vittorio Agnoletto, 'Diritto alla "privacy" e abusi nei confronti degli «utenti internet" di "INVESTICI"', question before the European Parliament, 12 July 2005, https://www.autistici.org/ai/crackdown/stampa/ interrogazione_parlamento_europeo.

'Therefore', the article read, 'all of the defense's strategy is already available to the prosecution: documents, analyses, records, and findings still not presented at trial. Forget about the secrecy of investigation and the right of defense.'[129]

Courtesy Visits to Aruba 2.0

The first Autistici/Inventati countermeasure was to withdraw the machine, clean it, and put it back online. It was an emergency intervention that completely resolved the matter by the end of June, when the fundamental services were reactivated.

It was a bitter pill to swallow. All of the good practices and technical mastery weren't enough to protect the privacy and anonymity of their nearly 30,000 subscribers – nor of the administrators themselves.

To recover the computer, a joint expedition of Autistics from various provenances was spontaneously organized. Essentially, anyone who could leave home without warning joined the caravan. Mille, for example, recounted that at the time he was working for a company that he could leave in hurry without too many problems. Ale remembers having noticed for the first time that Aruba was based on a street named after Sergio Ramelli, that is to say a 'fascist martyr'. This was a particularly disturbing fact which no one would have focused on in a different situation.

To collect the server, at least three cars filled with enraged people showed up. To avoid any misunderstandings, they were accompanied by a lawyer. A couple of people and the lawyer went into Aruba's office. The rest of the collective waited in the street, in the deserted parking lot where every once in a while three men in black glasses peered out at them from a car. After driving around in front of the Autistici, the car stopped at Aruba's entrance, turned around once more and disappeared onto the highway. After a while it returned. And continued like that for the rest of the visit.

Meanwhile, the discussion inside was long and irritating. The owner clumsily tried to explain himself, only worsening his position in the astonished eyes of the collective. There were moments of tension. Some insults were exchanged but in the end they were at least able to leave the company premises with the server in their arms, having dealt with the most urgent issue.

The computer was wiped and restored, then temporarily placed where ECN had their machines. Subsequently the judge ordered the police to destroy the data they had copied from the disks, so it couldn't be used (at least officially) in the courtroom. However, the problem of where to locate the server remained unchanged.

ECN benefited from being on an older contract, but the hosting costs for A/I's server were now unreasonable. For this and other reasons, it wasn't a sustainable solution. These moments of excitement also tested the policy of keeping the backups on another machine, in an unequipped place in the middle of nowhere.

---

129 SupportoLegale, 'Comunicato di SupportoLegale', *Autistici*, June 2005, https://www.autistici.org/ai/
crackdown/comunicati/comunicato_supporto_legale.

Besides, the result of relying on a home connection is that it never works. It was a difficult and delicate moment. It had already been decided that it was necessary to revolutionize the infrastructure, but the situation continued like this for a few months, waiting for the execution of Plan R*.

Plan R*

Plan R* put in place a network of self-managed servers, defined as a 'resistant communications network'.

Ale: *The terms are obviously incorrect: 'network' is a stupid way to say that there's more than one computer, and to convey that we were moving from a material structure to an immaterial one. The idea wasn't to disappear and become untraceable, which is hard and also a bit pointless, but to make it really complicated to bypass us. And we did it using sufficiently tortuous technical solutions. This way, if someone wants some of our data, they have to deal with the Investici Association.*

A/I wanted robustness for at least two reasons: technical and political. First, the new server network minimized the risk that the structure as a whole could suddenly collapse, leaving everyone stranded without a way to communicate. Secondly, it enabled A/I to support a universe of people who were resisting uniformity and control – a world of ideas that needed tools in order to spread and flourish.

Bomboclat: *Our customary paranoia may seem exaggerated but it usually turns out to be fortunate. At the end of the Aruba affair we had just the one machine, but from then on there's an exponential increase in the number of servers. And as that was not enough, other countermeasures would later be put into place to limit the damage that occurs from time to time…*

As we've seen, when Ale joined the collective at the end of 2002, A/I was already looking to redesign its infrastructure and make it more secure and resistant to downtime or outages. His arrival on the scene was crucial.

Cojote: *What we were discussing seemed very smart to me. I believe that Ale was mainly intrigued by the technological challenge and the opportunity to give what he did a social meaning. Together we built something that seemed very timely. How this then became Plan R* depended on a number of factors, and it was the years of work afterwards that determined how it turned out. That's how it went. Once the weak points of the infrastructure were identified, we all worked towards the solution.*

In response to the 2005 Aruba crackdown, it was decided that it was time to make these discussions tangible. The collective devoted itself to an engineering effort to finish it in the shortest time possible. It was a summer of hard work.

Gio: *I joined A/I at a fun moment: during the crackdown. So I took part in putting Plan R* into effect, even if they already had pretty specific ideas about what was to be done. We experimented with different things during this period: Autistici's first Tor node, a service that over the years has come and gone; Jabber, for instant messaging; the first draft of a certification authority that wouldn't need third party validation…*

But beyond the technical push, Plan R* really demanded political and strategic effort. Once it was decided that they couldn't possibly have machines only in Italy, they needed to figure out in which countries they could be located.

Bomboclat: *Where to put the tool itself? After the experience of Aruba, no one wanted to take unnecessary risks and it's essential that the people holding the machines be trusted. Such peace of mind can only be guaranteed through directly knowing the comrades responsible for the servers. Here the contacts acquired outside of Italy during the internationalist undertaking that was Indymedia prove to be very useful.*

Indymedia had served as global connective tissue, fostering by its nature a sort of militant internationalism. It had an in-built radio bridge to other countries, a connection that allowed groups even very far from the antagonist area to meet and coalesce.

Bomboclat: *For example we organized the No Border[130] camps with Indymedia, events where Italian hacklabs with their own identity, ethics, and needs, met people from a Belgian internet cafe who were inspired by completely different principles. Both recognized each other as brothers with a shared commitment to specific goals.*

Through this and other similar efforts, Indymedia not only acknowledged the historical significance of each different European political group, but also gave them a new boost and continuity, and provided or strengthened the contacts that later proved to be a great help.

Bomboclat: *In reality Plan R* had been ready for a year, at least since Ale and Phasa went to Brazil for the fourth Debian Conference, where they met the Americans from Riseup.*

In 2006, when the new structure had been active for a year, Blicero and Ale undertook a long trip to Scandinavia. That summer they crossed half of continental Europe by car. Their destination was Norway, but it was a journey with many stops.

Ale: *In Oslo we met the person who hosted our Norwegian server. Then we went to Germany, France, the Netherlands… it was a tour for socializing, we went to present Plan R* and at the same time meet people from the various backup communities that had made it possible!*

During the 7000-kilometer trip the two made numerous stops to present the infrastructure to various international groups similar to A/I, though none of them adopted a comparable approach.

Blicero: *Among our various international contacts, few followed our path. This is in part due to the fact that they have less users and their projects are of smaller size. With the Americans from Riseup, our relationship is stronger because their community isn't as small and the scale of their problems is similar to A/I's.*

In brief, with Plan R* the collective turned a new page, even if the internationalist impulse was quickly limited to the mere management of technical issues. Besides, there was a linguistic problem attributable to the difficulties in dealing with the dominant English-speaking world.

---

130 No Border: A network born in 1999 to show solidarity with migrants, campaign for freedom of
      movement, and fight deportations from the EU.

Alieno: *When we say 'Autistici' around the world, no one understands. The world speaks English and the Italian names of our domains are crippled because of it... We can't find a solution! For Plan R* we spent a while bogged down on the domain name that would let us overcome the Autistici-Inventati dualism. It was a bit of drama. We chose 'onenetbeyond' (but luckily then we haven't had to use it except for the launch campaign) together with English words containing the R:* R*esist, cR*ypto, oR*gasm, *that have almost come to equal +kaos!*

In October 2005, the multiplication of servers occurred, from one to a geographically distributed many, making use of a series of technologies later described in the Orange Book.

Roughly speaking, the basis for the new structure lies in the interchangeability of servers. They are configured identically and this makes them individually replaceable. None of them are essential.

The servers are then synchronized and the communication between them and outside traffic is encrypted.

But although the machines are functionally identical, the data they host is different. People's sensitive data, for example their email boxes, are distributed so that at any moment they can be moved to another server. This is very useful when the server they originate from becomes compromised, as events in Norway would soon show.

Plan R* wasn't conceived to back up and restore data, but rather to ensure that the structure as a whole would continue to function even when under attack. This reflects the collective's political priority – to give everyone the possibility to communicate and circulate censored material.

Ale: *Fundamentally the aim is to guarantee that people will still be able to communicate, no matter what happens.*

2005 marked a momentous change for A/I, expressed not only in the new technical structure, but also in a change of political orientation. And as much as it accomplished – from the survival of the service to the emergence of non-techie abilities within the collective – it wasn't a completely painless transition.

With Plan R*, and in spite of itself, A/I became exactly what it didn't want to become: a movement provider. The initial idea wasn't for the multiplication of servers as much as the growth of new groups to manage them, but except for a few cases, that clearly didn't work. As a result, some people slowly withdrew from the project. Caparossa left during this period. Beyond the reasons noted above, their motives for leaving included the difficulty of sharing skills and technical knowledge within A/I. In the push for Plan R* they recreated a very obvious gap between those who were technically qualified, and had time to grow in this respect, and those who found themselves carrying out either unskilled labor or unable to contribute to the project at all. It was a classic problem which in some ways is a constant and still unresolved; only with time and the stabilization of the new structure did it begin to fade. With Plan R* the collective let itself embrace the role of movement provider, but tried to implement a structure that this time was purpose-designed and technically very different from the original. This expansion led to another class of citizenship on the internet.

Ale: *On the internet there exist various levels of protection for user data, based on the social class to which you belong... as also happens to be the case in offline society. Well that goes for the digital world as well: it's your economic category that makes the difference. The low end, where people pay a few euros for a domain each year, is home to all sorts of abuses. The commercial providers have hyper-compliant policies towards the powers that be and don't protect their clients from legal problems because these costs aren't covered by what they charge. They take down the site at the first complaint and you have to prove that a mistake was made. A general attacker with enough power could simply send a request letter or fill out a form, and it doesn't cost them anything to get your data. We couldn't change that, because it's the industry standard, so we reversed the problem. With Plan R* our technical structure is comparable to a medium-sized corporation or institution and therefore going through us has a cost. Even if this doesn't prevent anyone from messing with us, it discourages people from doing it on a massive scale and whenever they like.*

Download a Copy, Upload an Idea

Those who have never participated in a KAOS Tour nor seen one in action could think Autistici is a bunch of heartless hackers, concerned only with code, circuits, and networks.

But actually the collective also has a strong creative side and, given the number of musicians among them, there was often talk of touring the world as a band... But they could never agree on a musical genre – they played everything from electronica to grindcore – and in the end they preferred to sit in front of a monitor programming and administering machines.

Pbm: *Digital rights interested me because one of my other passions was music. At the end of the 90s, the relationship between artist and audience was brought into question and the discussion involved the digital environment very directly. As a matter of fact, we can say that with Napster's arrival – but regardless of what Napster actually did – there began a witch-hunt against downloading music. Within LOA's orbit many projects were born including one I liked a lot: at the end of 2000 there was an articulate campaign against the new copyright law, that foresaw among other things a tax on all blank media.*[131]

The musical inclinations of various members of A/I and the related interest in the free circulation of ideas and content were felt from the beginning of the collective's life. Primo Moroni's phrase that A/I chose as their motto – 'Share knowledge, without installing power' – referred not only to the use of Linux, but encompassed a whole series of other fields.

Pinna: *I've always made music, and I was interested in computers and slowly getting into hacking. At that time I had started using Linux so I came into contact with the free software perspective based on copyleft – which isn't just a negation of copyright! So we brought a project to life, Copydown, which unites the different tensions and experiences of DIY/no-copyright that are tied to rebellious politics and to self-production. These are the embryos of what would become the 'Free Content' and Creative Commons licenses, the attempt to transplant from the world of software what had been shown to be possible with Linux and the GPL license. We also started documenting the phenomenon of file sharing that was just being born but already appeared unstoppable.*

---

131 Tax on all blank media: The infamous 'bollini SIAE' required labels, sold by the SIAE, to be affixed to all CDs, DVDs, and Blu-ray disks for sale, purportedly as proof that they are legitimate product.

Copydown was born before Autistici/Inventati and was previously hosted on another independent server, Strano Network, which originated in the BBS period and was especially popular in Tuscany.

Pinna: *Initially Copydown moves onto A/I as a guest and then slowly grows within it, also because of the turnover of people from Copydown who were more active promoters of the project. It moves progressively deeper inside Autistici and the two projects grow together. Although born from the needs of a very specific environment – that of music, textual, video, or in any case cultural production – Copydown has many similarities with the experience of Autistici and those which Autistici try to support.*

Copydown soon became the main platform nationally regarding free licenses, the circulation of knowledge, and free culture. Many debates that developed inside of Copydown were of shared interest to Autistici: interest in the latest technological discussions, the critique of patents, and the promotion of free software. And then there were the causes it shared with older movements, like DIY, that came from punk.

Pinna: *Filesharing for example was already a theme within Copydown and this connected it closely with important aspects of Autistici. Both because it addressed court decisions involving the seizure of servers or users' computers – often resulting in defeats for the major film and music multinationals – and because the software for P2P technologies is inherently linked to privacy and anonymity – things that are Autistici's everyday fare.*

Copydown's presence inside A/I proved increasingly logical because if the former wanted to promote no-copyright and copyleft, the latter was the go-to digital hub for social centers, political groups, and cultural associations that made use of these types of production.

But what did Copydown do? In the beginning it did research above all else. It followed the various proposals for licenses for the free distribution of software and other cultural products, proposals that were periodically explained on the website and discussed on the mailing list.

Pinna: *Before Creative Commons there were free licenses inspired by free software but applied to artistic works such as the Open Publication License, or the Free Art License. We didn't work a lot with these licenses. We just wrote articles providing an overview of them. Some were simply adaptations of software licenses to cultural contents, others were distinctly politicized. For example, there was one that banned use by the military – the SLUC software license[132] – and another that forbade use in the infringement of human rights or surveillance of users – the HESSLA.[133] After the rise of the Creative Commons, these licenses sort of vanished into thin air…*

What Copydown did was to find, translate, compare, and publicize the existence of these licenses to their audience of creators, DIYers, and distributors.

Pinna: *These are the people we have always addressed: a musician or small band that decide what to do with their own creations and how to do it; the label that brings musicians together*

---

132 The SLUC software license: From the Spanish Software Libre para Uso Civil ('Free Software for Civilian Use').

133 Hacktivism Enhanced-Source Software License Agreement.

and perhaps proposes they adopt a certain approach to social spaces also through these licenses; the groups inside of these spaces that distribute music and organize concerts, in an ongoing dialogue with both types of people – the creators and distributors.

When at the end of 2002 the Creative Commons licenses appeared, this new challenge to the world of copyright was immediately welcomed, but not without its own controversies among the participants of Copydown (because, frankly, there is no pure joy in this world!).

Pinna: *There was always a critical debate, like the discussions on the mailing list. And this reflected part of our backgrounds, because some of us came from programming and brought an approach founded on a legal mechanism via the GPL license, albeit modified so as to be more free (and this is the essence of the Creative Commons and other licenses); then there were those of us who came from the sphere of DIY, no-copyright, and the refusal of legality and copyright laws.*

Independent of the question of adopting or not a license and of recognizing the legal scheme, the needs of people using it remain the same: to have complete control of what they do and remove as many restrictions as possible to the freedom of distribution and circulation of content.

Within a few years, the Creative Commons licenses managed to get a toehold everywhere, supported by a strong international campaign and adapted to local legal systems.

Pinna: *In some ways the life of Creative Commons has somewhat reflected my involvement in this debate. At a certain point I saw these licenses had become a shared heritage and were now widely used, not just by those for whom the choice of how to make and distribute creative works was a crucial question. It had become established at a global level and at that point the motivation to raise awareness of this approach as an option, and the tools and licenses, waned. We had gotten the result we needed.*

Copydown was immediately defined as the 'Italian portal of No-copyright', but over time it grew and became an authoritative voice, in particular by putting online a number of resources, including a really unique archive of the music and texts of free culture.

The project also publicized itself through the organization of actions and protests, like those against software patents in 2005 and the assault on the Meeting delle Etichette Indipendenti (Meeting of Independent Labels, or MEI). On that occasion, a coalition of net-labels, web radios, musical groups, and independent activists belonging to the no-copyright/copyleft galaxy showed up uninvited to the festival and handed out a guide to no-copyright titled *RILASCIATI!*[134] Over the years Copydown was even able to hold their own event, with the provocative and ironic name: 'MAI'.[135]

Pinna: *One of the interesting things we did with (L)eft, the music scene around Copydown, was to organize a couple of MAIs, as an alternative to the MEI. We found ourselves among the bands and people who normally wrote on the mailing list and who came to see us in person, sharing the latest stuff, exchanging materials... At various times, when someone from Copydown was present, we distributed DIY material, released under a no-copyright or free*

---

134 Rilasciati: Word meaning both 'released' and 'release yourself'.
135 MAI: 'Never'.

license, together with materials with the same licenses downloaded from the internet and that we assembled and organized. Not everything was of the highest quality, but it was fair-trade certified from the copyleft point of view.

During the period when A/I was born, the digital world enabled many new forms of production and distribution, including video activism and web radio. Apart from Copydown, other projects took shape in those years. Among these was New Global Vision, or NGV.

NGV was born at the same time as Indymedia and A/I but had its own speciality: it offered a distribution tool to the video-activist community in the era of file sharing.

Zombi_J: *In the days after the G8 in Genoa, dozens of video tapes that were shipped from the media center arrived at the TPO in Bologna. With these materials, Indymedia people from different countries made* Aggiornamento 1, *that was immediately circulated both in traditional forms – VHS and CD – and uploaded via* FTP. *Within a few days that video was screened publicly on every continent, from Australia to the United States, from Japan to South America. The speed and relative ease of this process spurred us to anticipate that the distribution of video through the internet would explode in the months and years to come. Hence the inference that online tools would be needed to encourage this process, to enable distribution of productions from alternative circuits, both by activists and by non-activists.*

The project grew with support from the hacklabs and the movement's service providers, chiefly ECN and later A/I.

Zombi_J: *It was Void who dedicated himself to the coding, he did the first CMS which went online in 2001 on ECN's server before moving onto A/I some years later. But the videos were uploaded to four or five FTP servers in different locations to guarantee continuity of access in case of problems, and to spread the bandwidth and maintenance costs.*

Many from Autistici/Inventati embraced the project and made their skills available for the community, even if those contributions weren't always appreciated.

Bomboclat: *Whilst solving problems tied to the hardware in LOA, which was often unsupported, we set up a Linux video bank. No one ever used it for a finished production. We said, 'it works'. And they didn't use it. We were the ones who said, 'computer technology is beautiful, and if it's free that's even better. Always'. For them it was, 'whatever shit will let me immediately finish the video that I have to upload is useful. No matter what'. So between the video activists and the hackers, we could cordially go fuck ourselves. Often the video makers, being women, overcame our hate with a smile.*

NGV, in addition to publishing video, indexed a lot of metadata about the work: information on authors, related viewing suggestions, navigation paths; it also offered users the chance to comment.

Zombi_J: *The system was perfected in the following years and Ale radically innovated the uploading and organization of the FTP servers, migrated the site to A/I and launched a beta version with streaming.*

If the collective was always tiny from a strictly technical point of view, it was widely loved and used by a lot of video makers/media activists.

Zombi_J: *Videos arrived through various channels, by upload, by hand, or sent by traditional mail. So the first online video archive of the movement (and not just the movement) came to be.*

NGV archived almost seven hundred videos dealing with the widest range of topics and genres, from seminars on free software to short fiction films and theatrical performances. It also succeeded in recovering movement material of historical value, and more.

Alieno: *The first time I handed a copy of NGV's entire archive to some pirate TV station (I don't remember which), the 'package' comprised dozens of CDs, rigorously organized and labelled. A few years later, given the volume of the archive, I found myself delivering dozens of DVDs. Then I started to keep an updated copy on a USB hard drive and transfer the archive directly to the PC of whoever asked for it.*

The project over the years has involved a mixed community, that goes from simple users and neophyte video-makers to experimental documentary pioneers like Alberto Grifi.[136]

NGV worked alongside dozens of video collectives and pirate TV stations; it was often invited to present its model of production and sharing around Italy and internationally, and its contribution was recognized with a Prix Ars Electronica in Linz in 2005.

Zombi_J: *NGV was active more or less until 2007, after which the energy for the project faded. A series of technical and human resource problems brought the project to a halt although the online archive was maintained. A shame. As far as I'm concerned, it remains one of the best experiences in the realm of media activism.*

In 2002, after a series of initiatives in LOA entitled 'Fatti la Radio in Casa' (Make a Radio Station at Home), radio.autistici.org was born. The site was meant to empower anyone to try out audio streaming, and to provide users with a navigable list of existing and accessible projects.

Bomboclat: *The experience of Indymedia and the media center made us understand how useful it could be to relay the movement's radio stations so they could receive updates from the street. We understood that it was important and that this type of news coverage was to be given visibility (along with the streams of those who decided to make their own radio stations, of course).*

Among the various independent servers that adopted the project was Teknusi, who provided independent communications in the entire southern region of Campania.

ManO: *The thing that interested me and that I loved the most was the discussion about streaming audio for radio on the web. This thing seemed incredible to me… Imagine somebody in Naples who discovers radio over the web… clearly in the other cities they were already there, but this was the thing that interested me most. Autistici provided the icecast service, however they never put a lot of resources in this project.*

Teknusi also provided support for other radio stations when they transmitted the news from particularly important events.

---

136   Alberto Grifi was an independent filmmaker and documentarian. His films chronicle key moments of the 1970s counterculture from the free festivals to the anti-psychiatry movement.

ManO: *Streaming needed a lot of bandwidth and so we put up a server for that. We've gotten some pleasure from our services both at the local level and internationally, like when a few years ago we mirrored the streams from the G8 in Germany. More recently, there were the protests against trains carrying reprocessed nuclear waste in Germany last November, and we provided the Germans with useful support, relaying all of their audio streams. This made us also understand that we'd done things correctly, because at times there were two thousand simultaneous listeners and everything worked.*

Not all the changes the internet brought were as instantly positive as radio, however, a problem that soon affected members of Copydown's milieu and especially (L)eft, their musical wing, was dealing with social networks.

Pinke: *It was the year of the Myspace boom in Italy. It was initially noticed that the entire musical DIY scene – hardcore punk, electronica, whatever – was on Myspace. Facebook didn't exist yet or it wasn't famous at least, so everyone was there and it seemed that it had changed the destiny of tiny unknown bands who overnight could tour worldwide, which by the way was true, it was actually useful in some way. So suddenly everyone was catapulted onto Myspace, they had discovered this world. You found bands there that were unbelievably rebellious and unbelievably radical, but they had their nice little pages (illegible, generally) on Myspace.*

However, Myspace was a commercial platform in the hands of media mogul Rupert Murdoch, and more than a little incompatible with the vision of Copydown, (L)eft, A/I, and the entire DIY milieu. The problem was, when a few people were invited to the 2006 DIY Fest organized by people around Radio Black Out in Turin to talk in depth about social networks, they realized they couldn't offer an alternative. The commercial platform worked and was useful, people wouldn't stop using it out of principle.

Pinke: *With a few people from the DIY scene (I remember those from Turin and Rome in particular) we started to ask ourselves how we could make people aware of the fact that Myspace wasn't really the most revolutionary space. Possibly to change their minds, or at least open a non-commercial space that felt like it was theirs. Then the idea came to us to create a DIY portal on Autistici, something self-managed, where labels, groups, the whole world of DIY could find a way to publicize itself, maybe even form a community, by managing their own tools. No one from Autistici wanted to completely ban Myspace, to say that everyone had to have just a space on A/I. But it was paradoxical that this important scene had no existence on Autistici.*

So, for the next two years, while Copydown and (L)eft carried out the work of carefully analyzing and documenting the functioning of Myspace, a collaboration began between them and several bands towards the construction of autoproduzioni.org.[137] The result was the creation of the portal and a long document, titled *Uscire da Myspace (Leaving Myspace)*, where it explained chapter and verse the twisted mechanism underlying the social network.

Pinke: *Like a lot of other commercial services on the internet, Myspace is apparently free, but in reality we pay a lot for it. We pay for it not only through the advertising banners we see, but above all with the data that we, our friends, and fans send with every click on Myspace,*

---

137 Autoproduzioni: DIY-productions.

data that is accumulated and forms larger webs of relationships. This way we give a large multinational the possibility to analyze and control our tastes and friendships, to sell the results to the highest bidder and, in the end, to construct a world of advertising custom made for us.

Autoproduzioni.org didn't try to imitate Myspace. Rather it wanted to present itself as an aggregator for news about Italian and international DIY music.

Pinke: *We worked on it a fair bit. It used a CMS or something like that and there were categories and so on. In the portal's heyday there were many different subcategories, even non-musical DIY productions like book publishing.*

The idea was to make use of RSS feeds and make a portal by aggregating the feeds from sites already in existence, generating a kind of platform where you could find everything in the world of Italian DIY music. However, everything else remained at an embryonic level. It was never able to truly catch on. Reconstructing the structure of a social network was theoretically possible from a technical point of view, but it would have been pointless. The platform would have remained empty because of a lack of a critical mass, given that it needed a lot of contributors in order to take off.

Gio: *Social networks can be offered by anyone. Someone offers you a tool and thus a seed is planted. The seed is given to the people and grows as a function of people's actions. What can change is how these tools are promoted. There are as many different ways as there are goals... But social networks exist because you exist, otherwise they would be empty boxes, with many levers and buttons. But if no one pushes the buttons, the tool dies there.*

Also starting from these DIY experiences, the collective started to reflect on the opportunity to offer tools that supported this watershed moment and the more social implications that the web was taking on.

They started to talk about offering a blog platform to complement their websites, but the process took a long time, more than a year, because of the lack of software suitable to the political needs of the collective.

Pinke: *Autoproduzioni.org was a first experience and perhaps facilitated the process for us, in that we'd had an experience that had led us to understand how to set up the next shot. But at the level of user experience I think it wasn't really useful to many people because it had very little resonance. It continued to be an effort on our part. We wanted it to be a shared and collective effort. But it didn't turn out like that.*

The arguments and experiments on social networks continued. In the autumn of 2006, the blog platform Noblogs, or better yet, No(b)logs – blogs without logs – was launched.

Pinke: *Years later, Noblogs gave a new boost to the community, the users themselves are involved in the project. Before Noblogs there was a list of sites on A/I. There was no interaction: what you had was a simple public list including every single project. There were attempts at networking, but they were more limited. Now there's a network and you can exchange contacts and opinions with other people through it.*

No(b)logs

By 2005, the blog was a tool that had already been widely used for years, even if primarily for online diaries. Apart from a couple of exceptions proving the rule, the blogosphere still wasn't recognized as a valid information source. Until then there had never been a need to establish a blogging platform for the Italian movement, which in any case already had other established communications channels linked more strictly to their own social contexts. But given a bit of time, things began to change.

Alieno: *It's not by chance that all the old mailing lists disappeared and didn't reopen if they weren't tightly tied to a specific project. Originally, the mailing lists were background chatter but they gave you the possibility of going deeper. What is apparent also in other contexts largely dedicated to computers, is that the breadth of discussion somehow isn't there any more. The quantity of news flowing over us every day has increased a lot, so it's even more difficult to find moments to stop and think.*

Inside A/I the discussion about blogs unfolded on many levels. Although at the time the collective considered blogging to be essentially a private vice, it didn't pass them by that the political panorama was evolving and the movements, or 'the movement of movements', was at a low ebb. A brief historical analysis was enough to suggest that a phase of retreat and fragmentation had started and, from the point of view of digital tools, the transition to a latticed structure like blogs appeared as the most immediate way to capture and express the few remaining energies of the movement.

Bomboclat: *Noblogs only came into being as Indymedia weakened, until then the latter was given priority in the movement's media plans. During the transition of Indymedia from being organized nationally to being composed of local groups, many people who had previously loved it abandoned the project. The blogging platform was therefore also conceived to gather these authors and maintain some continuity. Our idea was that this tradition of critical content production shouldn't just get scattered around the net.*

Before the launch, the collective had to confront a series of difficult questions, including the fear that the platform might remain unused and that A/I as a wider community didn't exist.

Pinke: *I believe the establishment of a community is a slow thing. But it's here, I see a community.*

The discussion lasted months. It would take as long again to find the right software, but in the end the new project was born.

Obaz: *I no longer remember the reasoning that led us from autoproduzioni.org to the proposal of something for the whole movement, but it was a need that was in the air and discussed at almost every meeting. As often happens in the collective, I think there were a series of drives to innovation that come about only when there is the right software.*

In October 2006, Noblogs was finally launched. A/I passed from having a list of hosted sites to a platform of interactive content, aimed at producing 'useful networks'.

Obaz: *In the beginning, a network was supposed to be born from a home page consisting of various sections – recent posts, most read posts, latest blogs created, etc. – intended to publicize what was happening on Noblogs. Obviously that wasn't enough, so Ale invented this thing – what we would later refer to as 'bubbles' – with which you could see what people were discussing on various blogs, know how many people were using a keyword, in which posts it was occurring, etc. Ale and Blicero wanted to launch a revolution with these bubbles!... But then everything got stuck during the graphic implementation and the project was never finished. Every now and then we return to it and maybe we'll eventually get it done. Anyway, today you can follow blogs with feed readers and via social networks so I don't know if it would be something really useful.*

Contrary to pessimistic expectations, the users responded enthusiastically. By setting up a network, the collective had proof that there existed a small community around A/I, and that it was growing. Or rather Noblogs was helping it along.

Obaz: *In the beginning there was just us and a few friends. Today there are 3090 blogs. This evolution is difficult to narrate as it would require research in itself. In these five years many things have happened.*

What A/I provides is essentially an empty container, a tool to navigate the different individual voices. And seductive soviet-style graphics.

Alieno: *The number of people working on graphics became progressively smaller. By 2005, I was practically alone. For Noblogs, the inspiration came from Void, throwing out words with a typeface similar to Cyrillic, some pro-soviet stuff. Having played for years with subvertizing, I began to modify propaganda images from the Stalinist era and beyond. Given the good response to them, I created a whole series of images, some distributed as posters, some as stickers. In 2007, they ended up in a show on Do It Yourself culture curated by the Academy of Fine Arts of Carrara.*

Alieno's images brightened a memorable campaign, not least because Noblogs represented a definite advance as regards the refinement of A/I's communication style. Considering that for its first year and a half the collective had remained virtually unknown, due to an exclusive concentration on the technical aspect of its work and the implementation of services, the launch of something like Noblogs was an epoch-defining event.

Continuing a tendency born with Plan R*, they then put to work people previously confined to the back rooms to study Unix. Amidst the emergence of a communications and content practice, these less technical people bloomed, finding a more suitable role for themselves inside the group.

Obaz: *I entered the collective in January 2005. At the first meeting I attended Ale presented Plan R* in detail. I joined knowing that I would do what I could do – for example I think I translated half of the English version of the site. Actually, I now feel that I'm partly doing editorial work. I don't write a lot of the communiques because there are better writers within the collective with an ironic edge that I lack. Let's say that in my own small way I try and coordinate our communications, by translating texts or putting together newsletters when we decide to produce them. For Noblogs I can also help out on the technical side because it's easy: it's a CMS with an administration panel – I don't have to write any code. I can help the users and explain how the platform works.*

With Plan R* the idea that everyone should do everything was quietly abandoned and this was a pity. But because of how things have evolved, there are always new non-technical tasks through which to participate in the collective – from the management of the Paypal account financing the project to the translation and the bureaucracy of the renewal of hosting contracts.

Alieno: *Initially they insisted that everyone had to do everything. At a certain point, for example, Caparossa turns up at my house, partitions my laptop, slaps Linux on it, and says, 'Look, now you're a systems administrator. On this machine you have the root password'. And for the first couple of months I logged on in a cold sweat, because I was wondering, 'what am I going to break now?'*

Even today A/I's internal training process produces remarkable results: twenty-something system administrators manage the same machines without murdering each other.

Ale: *Let's say that even probing the most extreme depths of shared system administration you can't find anything similar. The maximum number of sys admins you can find anywhere else is five.*

It's not surprising therefore that the reallocation of tasks represented a difficult moment, because of the unique nature of the collective and its capacity to involve everyone in the work.

Bomboclat: *In the beginning those who agreed to assume a less technical role still had some difficulty interfacing effectively with the techies and there were a few frustrating episodes.*

But the period of discomfort didn't last long. The types of problems needing solutions were growing constantly and the tasks to be done were multiplying, so everyone found a space in which to best demonstrate their expertise. There was also a growing awareness of the value of each participant's commitment and of the relevance of the project; it had to go on no matter what, even more so in a period of decreased political activity and fragmentation.

Alieno: *What I miss today are the spaces and occasions of critical discussion. There aren't many environments where you can read or listen to arguments from people you don't know personally. If I think back to the beginning, when I was concerned with cyber-rights, I remember an environment rich in stimulation. Dozens of people comparing ideas, fighting, and pissing each other off. Finding that level of debate is now difficult. I think that some of the communities that have arisen around blogs, including those on Noblogs, can be laboratories of interesting ideas. It seems to me that we've all somehow developed attention deficit disorder and I've started to think that this result might have been intentional and was somehow planned. On the other hand, Autistici isn't the solution – we do other things. Luckily, we do other things. We try to provide tools to the community but not solutions for the complexity of communication, which should be developed collectively.*

At the time of the new platform's launch the transformation of the net accelerated and became more exciting, and discussions became increasingly lively. A/I is mainly a mechanism of strategic utility, and shortly afterwards it made available a service for instant messaging, Jabber, and the shared bookmarking system, Lilith, to meet the new needs of users.

In conclusion, Noblogs wasn't only a roll of the dice that became an unexpected success. It was a breakthrough on every front, because in some way it prevented A/I from becoming obsolete, opened new roads, and in the following years allowed the collective to continue offering the tools for anonymity and confidentiality which we know so well.

PART 3: FROM 2006 TO 2011
RECENT YEARS OR
BEFORE THE WORLD CHANGED

Setting the Scene, 2006-2011

At time of writing in late 2011, the last American troops are withdrawing from Iraqi territory, a country which analysts would de facto define as 'destabilized' and without a credible government. The search for arch enemy Osama bin Laden ends, not in Iraq or Afghanistan, but instead somewhere in Pakistan. Images of his body reawaken memories of that absolute evil which held court on the front pages of the newspapers ten years earlier in a world now enmeshed in other matters. The conflict in Afghanistan, however, is ongoing.

Meanwhile there has been an economic crisis, a deepening of the trend whereby western markets stagnate while those in the east explode – especially in China and India – and the eruption in both the debt and banking crises.

In Italy the long decade of Berlusconi has come to an end: the government is reshuffled under pressure from international finance and the European institutions. A technical government is formed under the leadership of Monti,[138] an honest broker in the eyes of the European Central Bank (ECB). But we are still in the middle of all this and it is not clear how things will turn out. Futile thus to talk of it here, in what is thought of as a contribution that deals with recent history rather than a narration of current events. Perhaps the twentieth anniversary of A/I will see us write of a European government led by the board of the ECB and directed by the Troika.[139] Before the full extent of the crisis was revealed and monopolized all attention, the politics of emergency had already imposed their rhythm on our existence. From the dishwashers to sweet wrappers, from beggars to the weather forecasts: in our odd world the sky constantly threatens to fall on our heads. This continuous emergency has been skillfully mixed with a fresh wave of racism so that immigration was quickly made to rhyme with invasion, Moroccan with drug dealer, Senegalese with prostitute and so on. The first outcome of this poisonous climate is stigma: figures are created on whom the fears and insecurities of an entire society can be focused. While this process is common throughout history, our world of media overexposure and 'speed up' changes the characters on a daily basis; though this verges on the ridiculous, it drives a spiral of anxiety that feeds itself.

Meanwhile the failure of the wars instigated by the USA, and the fracturing of the fragile but efficient ideological apparatus built up to support them, has given legitimacy back to critical voices. And to this is added the economic crisis which hits the crazed capital of international finance. In fact dissident voices had never really disappeared, if anything they had grown louder, but had objective difficulty attracting attention in the deliberately confused climate of permanent emergency. But 2010 and 2011 have been years of re-emergence for social

---

138 Mario Monti: Italian economist and politician. He was made prime minister at the end of 2011 in order to address the Italian debt crisis.
139 Troika: The International Monetary Fund, European Commission, and the European Central Bank acting together.

movements and a reawakening of civil society. In Italy a broad front is formed in defense of common goods and with a fairly coherent criticism of the neoliberal model. The No TAV movement goes through important days in the Susa Valley, students launch the Onda (the Wave), a national protest against educational reform. More generally the deterioration of living conditions in the West provides a stimulus for the creation of dynamic grassroots structures. All over the world people return to the streets, from the Indignados[140] to Occupy Wall Street,[141] and strikes and demonstrations everywhere. Again it is impossible for us to know where this new process will bring us, whether it will exhaust itself in the agony of existence, extinguished by another downturn, if it will be crushed and repressed or if it heralds a resuscitated social consciousness capable of imposing its will on the economy and politics. Probably all this will happen, and lots more besides; maybe it would be wise to organize ourselves in a timely manner. The dilemma of our funny post-postmodern world was aptly synthesized by Kurt Vonnegut in his novel *Galapagos*: 'In this era of big brains, anything which can be done will be done – so hunker down.'

Hacktivism, 2006-2011

As the new millennium's first decade progressed we got a better grasp of the interests at play on the chessboard of the network. The internet appeared destined for two principal uses: moving information and building community. With the end of the pioneer phase and the arrival of large investors alongside hundreds of millions of users, these questions are now on the table and are imbricated in a rather complex dialectical process, in a becoming where the outcomes are neither obvious nor to be taken for granted.

TV and print media have been supplemented and in part replaced by social networks and streaming platforms – the music and film industries have to reckon with file sharing in all its forms. The monetary value of intellectual property has to be redefined, as well as its very meaning. This is not a painless process where it is clear which way we're headed: instead it's a battlefield. From 2006 onwards there have been continuous attempts to block peer-to-peer networks and impose liability on providers for materials circulating online. Periodically there are attempts to introduce legislative instruments which will enable the removal of content from the net, but none of this succeeds in marginalizing the phenomenon. In 2008 a case was taken against the Pirate Bay, a reference point for file sharing based on BitTorrent. But the amount of shared data has only increased and has ended up on so-called 'cyberlockers', platforms for the sharing of files directly on the web itself. As we write, the United States has seized Megaupload, one of the largest commercial suppliers of such services.

Here we are dealing with non-linear processes wherein opposing economic interests mingle with the desire of users to swap content, raising non-trivial issues of freedom of expression. In general the majority of governments do not view the uncontrolled circulation of information favorably – it often results in political embarrassment – but this contrasts with the interests

---

140 The Indignados: A civil movement for radical change addressing both the economical and political situation of its country; the Indignados is often considered an anti-austerity movement. Because it was born in Spain on the occasion of the elections of the 15 May 2011, it is also called the 15-M movement.

141 Occupy Wall Street: A protest movement concerned with global inequality, inspired by the recent exploits of the Indignados in Spain. The movement was born in September 2011, within the financial district of New York City, Wall Street. Protestors took over a square, Zuccotti Park, where they were able to remain until November. It launched the Occupy Movement.

of the major economic lobbies. In this sense they are all of a piece: from China to Iran and from the US to Italy. If Twitter is used to discredit the Iranian government then the US government supports it as a tool of democracy. On the other hand when it is used to coordinate the London riots in the summer of 2011 there are immediate demands for censorship and an outcry over the lack of legislative instruments to gag the network. In 2010 Wikileaks[142] played on this ambiguity based on the assumption that once on the Net all types of information are difficult to remove. In brief the players are both multiple and sufficiently powerful to create a situation which is complex and tricky to analyze. One can only find one's bearings somewhat through an assessment of the second characteristic of the net: community.

The internet not only functions as a container of information but also brings groups of people into contact. The so-called social networks have been built on this axiom, and today seem almost to have superseded the web, or rather have become the interface through which everything else is accessed. During 2006 the crisis hit Myspace just as Facebook, YouTube and Twitter were establishing a foothold. Once Google has been included we have probably mentioned everything that the majority of users today identify as the internet.

Once the net is formed, and without additional technological revolutions underway but with a large part of the global population involved, it is no longer the quantity of information that makes the difference but the channels in which it is circulated. Users tend to split themselves up into communities, inside which selected content circulates, filtered by interest. Whoever wants to sell you something, get your vote, your agreement, or simply your attention, will try and insert themselves inside your community or, better still, be the actual provider of it. What we have hitherto defined as hacktivism adapts itself to this. Each structure, A/I included, ends up either consciously or otherwise constituting a community in search of contact with similar groups. Hacktivism spreads throughout the net, and people open pages on Facebook, a Twitter feed, blogs on both Noblogs and Blogspot, mail both on Autistici and Gmail, upload videos of demonstrations to YouTube and photos to Flickr. With all of the advantages, problems and contradictions that this implies.

An extremely heterogeneous mix of groups and users are brought together in mobilizations against online censorship and repressive legislative proposals. The laws against file sharing involve everyone from politically organized groups to users who just want to be able to download free video games for their Xbox. On the other hand, the non-virtual part of the game grows steadily in importance. A community is of greater coherence and interest where it exists also outside of the web, if it is capable of meeting and sharing experiences, and intervening in the environment around it. The Hackmeeting community would not be what it is without its annual meeting, without members seeing one another and sweating together during those torrid summer days. A/I has made it through a decade because we still have the desire to meet up face to face and plan things together. As in the best moral pamphlets, we would like thus to conclude with a maxim borrowed from *A Man Without A Country*, another work by

---

142 Wikileaks: An organization distributing confidential documents online. Founded in 2006 by Julian Assange and unnamed others, the site describes itself as 'an uncensorable system for untraceable mass document leaking'. Despite the presence of wiki in its name, Wikileaks is not a wiki-style site open to user modification. In recent years it has moved to a system of journalistic co-production, acting as a source for raw information which is then collaboratively explored with established journalism organizations.

Vonnegut: 'Electronic communities build nothing. You wind up with nothing. We are dancing animals. How beautiful it is to get up and go out and do something. We are here on Earth to fart around. Don't let anybody tell you any different.'

A Collaborative Network

Notwithstanding the efforts of Plan R* to make the A/I network more robust against attacks, technical tricks alone are not sufficient. The strength of the project has been that of the community supporting it. The interpretation of the adjective 'social' within A/I tends decidedly towards the concept of mutual aid.

Obaz: *Noblogs became somewhat self-managed, also because ultimately you have your blog where you can also allow other people to create an account... There are manuals for the platform, people can study them and explain things to others. 'Femminisimo a Sud' ('Feminism in the South') got every feminist in Italy onto Noblogs and explained to them how it works technically through workshops. She organized a couple of seminars first on how to use Lifetype and then WordPress. Sometimes they got us involved, others they did on their own.*

Noblogs attracted a variety of specific communities, from feminists to anarchists, large and small groups which now bonded through action, promoting practices ranging from art to community gardens. Another notable aspect lies in how Noblogs maintained the internationalist heritage of A/I, so much so that the most read blog, annalist.noblogs.org, is in German.

Obaz: *Germans, Russians, Portuguese, South Americans – they all turned up on A/I. We had versions of the site in many languages, including a couple of pages in Chinese. The translation of the autistici.org and inventati.org website is due principally to the collaboration of individuals who started rewriting the pages in their own language.*

We have Russian because at a certain point several texts in Cyrillic arrived at info@; we tried to understand them using Google Translate, if only to work out if they were talking about the same stuff! And then we began to put our documents online in Russian because there was a volunteer who translated them from English. Then there's Nah, a Brazilian girl who we later got to know in person and who translated the site into Portuguese because she decided that she liked us...

Over the years various experiments were tried to help the users to collaborate with each other, to provide mutual assistance and give life to what could eventually be called a true community.

Psykozygo: *The decision to reopen the forum as a space for peer assistance between users was a truly unexpected success. There are many examples of collaboration between people, whether it's a matter of the visual customization of a specific blog or the resolution of small everyday problems linked to the mail client or other services.*

But collaborations are not only triggered via Noblogs. There is the case of Collane di Ruggine, a self-managed publishing project also co-produced by the collective.

Reginazabo: *Collane di Ruggine was born at the Hackmeeting in Pisa. Mostly there are three people involved, but lots of others subscribe to the project mailing list. We got to know one another through A/I, but everything began while chatting on Jabber when we discovered* *that we all liked to make books. The co-production with the collective happened because it sometimes supports other initiatives on the basis of affinity, even if they don't strictly speaking have anything to do with the technological agenda. If on the one hand it's true that inside the collective our views are not always the same, it is also the case that some practices and activities fit within the core of our culture.*

Initially the curators thought of a publishing project focused in some way on the use of technology. In fact the first work published was a version of a graduation thesis on the relationship between man and technics in the novels of J. G. Ballard. Over time however they realized that they had lots of short stories and in the end opted for a fanzine, *Ruggine*,[143] in which they publish illustrated fiction.

Reginazabo: *Our stories sometimes have a steampunk atmosphere, an imaginary which I think is highly suited to the historical moment. I believe that it manages to fascinate people and thus draw them into ideas they would otherwise never have come in contact with where you simply tell them the truth. The plain truth, that's it: in Genoa in 2001, I realized that the simple truth was not enough. When you just tell the truth they throw you in Bolzaneto[144] and beat the shit out of you.*

In recent years, and stretching beyond its narrow technical role, the collective has paid close attention and given support to some campaigns dedicated to social issues.

Reginazabo: *Between 2007 and 2008 we just couldn't deal with it any more in Italy. Our impression was that there was an attempt to conduct politics based on fear and moral panic, and that it was no accident that politicians and journalists were over-egging it: this was democratic racism at its maximum. I remember the story that broke the camel's back of my impatience: the Ponticelli pogrom in Naples when a young Roma girl was accused of kidnapping a baby and the next day the whole neighborhood attacked the gypsy camps from which everyone had to flee.[145] At the Hackmeeting in Palermo we were approached by some people who proposed that we jointly devise a project against surveillance and the social exploitation of fear. Seeing as there were also positive experiments which no-one was talking about, we thought of using an aggregator to bring them together and thus acquire greater visibility.*

Some of those with whom the collective began to work on the project were also running the 'Freedom not Fear'[146] campaign, sponsored by the EFF; their involvement was crucial because they encouraged A/I to take responsibility and do something.

Reginazabo: *We had just bought the domain 'anche.no',[147] just at the right time! First off we set up the blog paura.anche.no[148] and gave the password to a group of projects. Then we*

---

143 *Ruggine* (*Rust*): A collaborative, DIY, self-published magazine collecting steampunk oriented stories, and much more besides. The project is hosted on Noblogs: https://collanediruggine.noblogs.org/english.
144 See footnote 117.
145 The Ponticelli pogrom followed a campaign of hatred and exploded on the morning of the 12 May 2008. The incidents went on all day.
146 Freedom not Fear: International campaign for freedom of speech and against surveillance – http://www.freedomnotfear.org.
147 Anche.no: Literally 'also no'. It roughly translates as a sarcastic 'maybe not!'
148 paura.anche.no: 'Fear not!' or 'Fear? Maybe not'.

invited the same number again to participate. To a large extent our work was putting together the blog on the topic, but we also produced our own publications. For several months the portal functioned really well.

However the campaign did not finish there. On the contrary, it soon evolved into something quite unexpected. As they say, one thing is born from another, and so it was that in this same period the *Babau*[149] made its first appearance.

Bomboclat: Babau *is a spin-off from the collective, which beyond technology is as you know dedicated to the question of communicative forms. In this case it tried to hook into the 'Freedom not Fear' campaign by finding a communicative formula which would enable the deactivation of the strategy of fear and repression, at least at a conceptual level.*

It all began when Alieno took it upon himself to draw the essence of the politics of fear, the very incarnation of fear as a political instrument: the Babau. So it was that two eyes and a threatening mouth against a black background became the curious mascot of the campaign against fear.

Alieno: *Sometimes the simplest solution is also the most effective. I wasted weeks pondering how to draw fear and it was enough to strip it down to the essentials.*

The purpose of the portal paura.anche.no was actually to highlight positive projects from Italy whilst simultaneously ridiculing fear. And the Babau was needed for this purpose.

Bomboclat: *The idea was to invoke this nightmare of every child which finds a grotesque echo in the world of adults as a justification for law and order policies, not to mention the senseless paranoia which feeds upon the deterioration of the social context which they themselves generate: a vicious cycle which has enslaved us now for at least a decade in a completely disproportionate and intolerable manner. A way out of so much heaviness is offered in the lightness of this imaginary character, responsible for every evil imaginable, even for some which are distinctly improbable.*

The campaign took off and out of it a series of regional initiatives was born in Milan, Florence, Rome and Bologna, then in Pisa, Falconara, Padua, Turin and Parma...

Alieno: *The thing to remember in the Babau campaign is the coordination: the Babau showed up both in the big cities and small provincial towns in planned appearances, generating curiosity and triggering a virtuous cycle which continued autonomously for months.*

Eventually a call to arms was made: drawings and stories which illustrate that sense of anxiety that was feeding the emergency politics of the period. The many faces of the Babau were to be sought out.

Reginazabo: *At a certain point we got in touch with the Scuola Romana dei Fumetti, the Roman Comics School, from which there arrived various versions of the Babau: about forty illustrations on the theme of social fear, some from well-known artists. This then became an exhibition which toured all over Italy.*

---

149 Babau: In Italian folklore Babau is an imaginary monster, a 'boogeyman'. Typically, children are told to behave 'otherwise the Babau will come and get you'.

In addition to the traveling exhibition, the campaign also produced a book of postcards and short stories, inspired of course by the taunt of the Babau. The title: *The Babau. Fear of the Dark?*

Reginazabo: *The exhibition went as far as Berlin, it had its resonance. When we produced the book with Collane di Ruggine with the stories and illustrations, contributions even arrived from abroad written in Italian – it was just incredible!*

Legal Cases

Pedopriest, 2007

Why does it always have to happen in summertime? Is it the parliamentary recess? Or the end of the football championship? That will be for posterity to judge. In the meantime, let us reconstruct this umpteenth legal episode in which the collective was involved. An ugly incident of digital censorship and maybe even something more: a misunderstood work of net-art.

Luca à Volontè[150]

30 June 2007: a week after the release of his new video game *Operation: Pedopriest*, Molleindustria removes it voluntarily from the site[151] explaining that he doesn't want to create any trouble for their hosting provider, after a shitstorm has been set off in the Italian Parliament by the honorable Luca Volontè, MP. As soon as the funny new flash animation was launched, the UDC[152] MP made it his personal crusade and pressed a parliamentary question[153] where he demanded the government take immediate steps against *Pedopriest's* content, 'offensive to religious sentiments'. Not satisfied by this, he also suggested the prosecution of its authors for pedophilia offenses.

The response of the government was swift, and on the 28 June, during the session of the Chamber of Deputies,[154] the undersecretary Paolo Naccarato made it known that the removal of the web page from the server was ongoing. Molleindustria withdrew the game and denounced what happened: *Pedopriest* is clearly intended as a satire of the clergy, and is definitely not a child-pornography game. In this respect the game's splash page is unequivocal:

> Once again the Church is in the midst of controversies for the sexual abuses committed by the priests. The Vatican created a task force to prevent sinners from being captured and put on trial according to the secular states' laws. You have to control the operations: establish a code of silence and hide the scandal until the media

---

150 Luca à volontè: Luca a gogo, a joke based on the name of the MP.

151 Molleindustria, 'Operation: Pedopriest', website and video game, 2007, www.molleindustria.org/en/operation-pedopriest.

152 Unione Democratica di Centro (UDC): Union of Moderate Christians and Democrats, a minor but influential party at the time.

153 Interrogazione Parlamentare: Parliamentary Inquiry. A Parliamentary protocol enabling one or several deputies either to acquire information from the government/minister on a specific fact or a point of policy.

154 *Measures to counter the offenses against the religious feeling and against all denominations*: Title of the Parliament's response to the above mentioned inquiry by the UDC party.

attention moves elsewhere![155]

Pedopriest is not as scandalous as the news events it mocks. But how can a game devised to condemn the spread of pedophilia amongst the clergy become itself a victim of the laws against pedophilia? The honorable Volontè, clearly a genius of pranks and *détournement* himself, invoked the provisions on virtual pornography.[156] The law targets what are described as: 'virtual images [...] made with graphic techniques not derived in their totality or in part from real situations, and whose depictive qualities make appear as true situations which are not actually real.'[157]

Essentially, or arguably, the game could thus be considered illegal in Italy. The urgent parliamentary question obviously aims to protect the 'good name' of the clergy by blocking the distribution of the game.

Once news of the censorship spread on the net there was an immediate multiplication of mirrors, links to the game, and new sites where it could be downloaded; A/I hosted *Pedopriest* on its server; various blogs on Noblogs took part in the silent revolt in support of Molleindustria... with the result that deep in the night of the 2 July A/I's US-based server hosting Noblogs was shut down.

A (Hardly) Mysterious Organization for the Protection of Children

It's the power of the word: pedophilia. The most overplayed bogeyman – along with terrorism – waved under people's noses every time there's discussion of digital rights, anonymity online, privacy.

In this instance a mail was enough, or rather an allegation by a generic 'organization for the protection of children' of which no-one ever heard anything thereafter.

In fact, due to a series of laws passed in a majority of countries, in cases involving child pornography a notification (or an anonymous denunciation) is enough to have a site or a web page blocked: due to the seriousness of the crime, action is to be taken first and the facts checked later – if it turns out to be a false alarm everything is put back where it was before, with the most sincere apologies.

People became aware of what had happened on the morning of the 3 July, but it took a while to work out what was going on given the absence of any legal investigation of A/I or anything which would justify the suspension of the service. Then the facts began to emerge.

The collective had certainly expected a reaction but not that a mere telephone call from Italy could succeed in persuading a 'friendly' American provider to again shut down the whole of Noblogs just to take down one piece of content. On the other hand, an international call was all that was needed to resolve the matter.

---

155 Molleindustria, 'Operation: Pedopriest'.
156 The provisions on virtual pornography are covered by Law 38, passed on the 6 February 2006, http://www.camera.it/parlam/leggi/06038l.htm.
157 Italian Criminal Code, art. 600-ter, see United Nations Office on Drugs and Crime, 'Database of Legislation: Italy', https://www.unodc.org/cld/en/legislation/ita/codice_penale/libro_secondo/articles_600-600septies2/article_600ter-600septies2.html?.

The collective managed to contact the owner of the provider by telephone and explain the background. As a matter of caution it was decided to contact lawyers so as to avoid unnecessary risks and reactivate the platform as quickly as possible.

As soon as the provider received confirmation that *Pedopriest* did not infringe any law in the US, it plugged back in the server and Noblogs was back in action. Here is how the provider responded to A/I:

> We have reviewed the content you posted with the assistance of legal counsel that is familiar with United States law. The content is legal.[158]

With hindsight we could say that thanks to Plan R*, censored content was immediately back online and a brief blackout occurred only because of the difference in time zones.

Stubbornness

The *Pedopriest* affair didn't finish here. Two days later, on the 4 July, the website *Liberté, Egalité, Volonté*,[159] *The Blasphemous Art Riot* was seized. The site had been set up by a non-existent group called Les Liens Invisibles, supposedly in collaboration with the Image Guerrilla Group. It was one of the many irreverent web pages that emerged in solidarity with Molleindustria.

This time, articles 494 (impersonation) and 595/3 (defamation) of the criminal code were invoked as the grounds for seizure: the brilliant web page, a real piece of net-art, clones the layout of the deputy's website and lampoons its contents. Moreover, every link connects to a mirror of Molleindustria's *game, or to a web page containing a random press statement on censorship.*

It was another abuse of process, as we already know from the *Trenitalia* affair, and by the 10 July the site *Luca a Volontè – lucavolonte.eu –* was back online as well.

Orwell's Grandchildren

If at the outset the collective found itself having to interact largely with skeptics and technophobes, the increased use of the net together with the growth in the number of users has radically changed the scale of problems to be faced and the solutions to be offered.

As we have said several times, the defense of privacy is a key issue for A/I, but in the last five years it has also become a space for experimentation and a front line facing the advance of social networks.

Gio: *With the discovery of the Tor anonymizing service we could at last unleash the desire for anonymity online!*

Once again the collective was working to protect its members' privacy and anonymity.

---

158 Autistici/Inventati, 'God Bless America', *Cavallette blog*, 4 July 2007, https://cavallette.noblogs. org/2007/07/641.

159 Again, a joke about MP Volontè's surname.

Gio: *The existence of a Tor network relies on whoever installs the software on one or more computers with public connections and then makes them available to the network. It's a collaborative system, similar to a P2P network. This made it interesting from my perspective. Furthermore it is a tool with incredible potential in environments characterized by control and censorship.*

All new solutions are first studied and then only implemented after careful consideration by the collective.

Bomboclat: *As regards Tor we made an assessment of the risk. It's a very sensitive service in so far as the exit nodes often face legal charges and we did not want to compromise a network in which sensitive data – such as mailboxes – are present. We decided that it would be better if this service were to grow in parallel with our network. There was also a campaign 'Adopt a Tor Server' but it never really took off.*

The many years of commitment to privacy and anonymity online were recognized in 2008 when A/I won the 'Winston Smith – Privacy Hero' award, the only positive accolade amongst the Big Brother Awards. Just to brag (!), we reprint here the reasons for the prize:

> In the field of its activity the A/I collective has for years conducted an untiring and praiseworthy provision of communication services far more respectful of privacy than either commercial or institutional entities. It has done so both voluntarily and without charge, notwithstanding both economic difficulties and severe technological attacks, justified as the secondary effects of judicial inquiries. It has responded to such problems in a positive and creative manner and continues to provide the means to those who feel the need to protect and preserve their privacy online. With limited resources it has committed itself to the laudable attempt to build a communications structure resistant to the attacks of censors.[160]

Alieno: *Digital life in the time of web 2.0 filled itself with apparently indispensable applications. But the level of understanding of how they function has fallen simultaneously. On these questions there's a ton of work to be done and consciousness to cultivate... I prefer paranoia and skepticism as opposed to the rampant techno-fetishism which has now also extended to objects such as telephones, MP3 players, etc.*

Over the ten years of the collective's existence the issue of the right to personal privacy has not progressed, but rather has undergone a sea-change and this has driven A/I to question itself, study, seek out solutions, etc.

Obaz: *The lessons on privacy today have been forgotten. Before Facebook, the internet was used by nerds for fun and by others to send mail or to visit a particular website. Then it began to be entertainment. And when you say: 'Hey, this entertainment is dangerous' it's a bit like telling someone 'Hey, you know cocaine is bad for you'. I mean, you sound like my grandpa. So we need to find the right way to respond in this situation. It's a problem which we are still working on because it's no longer merely a technical question, nor was it ever. We discuss it often on the list, why some things work and others not.*

---

160 Big Brother Award Italia 2008, http://bba.winstonsmith.info/bbai2008.html.

From time to time, like in the alarming case of Facebook and its unstoppable expansion, A/I tries to conduct 'damage minimization' campaigns, conscious of the absence of any feasible alternative.

Obaz: *Since the beginning of Facebook the privacy problems of the platform were demonstrated in several areas. Twitter is less invasive, but I would prefer that our users use Identi. ca,[161] the open source micro-blogging equivalent. I write my tweets there as well, but everyone answers me on Twitter! There aren't enough people on Identi.ca. But then sometimes the opposite occurs. People get to know one another on Twitter and then switch to self-managed platforms. I've watched various projects originate like that and then open a blog with us. Or even move their own personal blog to us. I think that it's all connected to the question of OWS, Occupy Everything, the Spanish Revolution and the last year (2011). It happens in that moment when a group of people emerges who had their blog or Twitter feed just as a personal notebook and then began to network amongst one another. Doing so through the internet maybe they got in touch with other people who are more privacy-aware, so they exchange information and make a more conscious political choice of platform.*

For many people, from Russian dissidents to NGO workers operating in war zones, writing on Noblogs rather than on a commercial platform which does not guarantee their anonymity remains a real need rather than a gesture of belonging to some community. But the privacy question is decisive also for those with less adventurous existences.

Obaz: *The privacy issue is more relevant than ever. You just have to think of Nymwars which broke out around the policy of Google Plus which demoted pseudonyms, asking for the real name of the account user. This demonstrates that the possibility to use a nick unrelated to one's real name is still important for people and the tendency to use a pseudonym for one's virtual identity remains strong. But I don't think that it's as important for these people that their pseudonym never be connected to their real name: it's not about retaining anonymity. It's more about a vague consciousness than an in-depth analysis. But in web 2.0 people tend to apply common sense and I think people feel a little more protected through the use of a pseudonym. It's something which is also still of importance in the choice to use Noblogs.*

Also because of this today there's a bit of everything on Noblogs, also a few village idiots who are tolerated for the simple reason that they exist (or in the worst case with the policy that 'our laughter will bury them'[162]). There are those who have a real need for anonymity and those who just want to protect their privacy; there are those who think that it guarantees freedom of expression more than other platforms and those who choose it on the grounds that the project should be rewarded; finally there are those who use it so as to indicate their political alignment.

Obaz: *Like Mille in the days of info@, on Noblogs I've done a bit of proselytism and so I know its geography pretty well. I have a very movement-driven vision of the whole A/I project but Noblogs especially doesn't represent any specific political ideology. It goes without saying*

---

161 Identi.ca: Micro-blogging service. Conceived as an alternative to proprietary walled-garden services (like Twitter), identi.ca was based on StatusNet until 2013 and is now built off pump.io, a more general-purpose framework for federated social networking.

162 'Our laughter will bury you', 'Una risata vi seppellirà' in Italian: Slogan coined by 19th century anarchists defiant in the face of state oppression. For many years it has been the legend on a famous poster printed by Soccorso Rosso (Red Aid) which shows a turn-of-the-century worker being arrested by the police with a smile on his face.

that the social centers and the movements close to us use either Noblogs or some other non-commercial platform. But there are completely distinct projects which have opened their blogs on Noblogs who don't address political or movement-related questions. They write about whatever, so it's not just a platform for activists. For sure it's the case that someone who opens a blog there doesn't do so because it has a pretty name, but rather because they've thought some issues over and made a specific decision, otherwise they would never have discovered its existence.

Legal Cases – The Norwegian Crackdown

It is only to contest our theory of disruption as a summer phenomenon that we turn now to the most recent legal affair involving the collective; it occurred in the middle of a freezing winter.

For several hours on the 6 November 2010 Norwegian police seized Autistici/Inventati's server in that country and made copies of all its hard drives. Initially we understood only that the Norwegian cops were acting on the basis of an international request – obviously emanating from Italy.

Once again, in search of we know not what – in any case something connected to an individual or a couple of users – the privacy of thousands is potentially violated. Immediately on learning what had happened, the collective asked all its users to change the passwords of both their mail and their FTP server – an action required not only for those who had their mail on Contumacia (the server in question) but for everyone.

News of the search by the Norwegian police spread by word of mouth, via websites and blogs. Thanks to the Plan R*, which proved itself an excellent anti-censorship tool, all services were reactivated within two hours on another server. Within twenty-four hours the entire infrastructure worked perfectly again. As a precaution the collective's technicians moved all the mailboxes which had been on the seized machine to another server and thus it happened that those who had their mail on Contumacia lost access to it temporarily.

A reminder to all regarding 'good housekeeping': don't keep your mail archive online on A/I's machines, it's a habit which (as in this case) can prove to be a bad move. Although the drives are encrypted, it is not smart to trust blindly in technology – there are basic errors which can nullify strong cryptography. In conclusion, it is not wise to gamble with your own security by entrusting it to third parties, even if they happen to be A/I.

So apparently minimal damage was done. But it remained to be seen who was responsible for the violation of the server.

Recap: Casa Pound[163]

It turned out that everything had began on the 9 December 2008 in Avezzano, a large municipality in the Marsica region of Abruzzo.

For that was when a complaint was made alleging the intimidation and defamation of Gianluca Jannone, leader of the neo-fascist group Casa Pound, and Ercole Marchionni, founder of Casa Pound Avezzano.

The purported intimidatory and defamatory acts comprised: a slogan sprayed on a wall, some red paint on a doorbell and some posts made on abruzzo.indymedia.org and on orsa.noblogs. org where it was demanded that declared neo-fascist groups (like the one to which these two belonged) not be granted use of public spaces.

Based on this legal complaint the public prosecutor Stefano Gallo opened an investigation, and shortly afterwards the inevitable request for personal details reached the postal police[164] in Milan. Both the blog and the associated mailbox were hosted on A/I and the Investici Association (based in the Lombard capital) had to respond.

In August 2009 the Investici Association was asked to depose in the capacity of a 'person (sic) informed in the matter' and declared before public officials that on its servers there were neither logs related to the mailbox orsa@canaglie.net, nor records in connection with whoever set it up.

By the book.

Clearly unconvinced of the good faith of these declarations, the public prosecutor sent an international letter of request to Norway, Holland, and Switzerland, justified by an investigation regarding 'threats', in order to obtain from the providers hosting A/I's servers data which the collective did not have. In November 2010 the Norwegian postal police, pursuant to the letter of request, went to the offices of a provider who hosted an A/I server and cloned all the hard drives contained in the machine, whose contents (fortunately) were largely encrypted.

---

163 Casa Pound: Fascist organization which appeared in 2003 with the occupation of a building in the Esquilino district of Rome, known for its numerous immigrant population. Defining itself as a group of 'third millennium fascists', Casa Pound has organized its own campaigns around housing, campaigns against the banks, and educational reform. To a significant extent it has sought to contest fields of political activism traditionally viewed as the territory of the left. This modernized and superficially radical approach, combined with smart branding, has enabled Casa Pound to spread throughout Italy, and there are now social spaces aligned with them in many towns and cities. Where the far right has some influence on local politics, Casa Pound has also benefited from their tacit sponsorship, as was the case in Rome during the period while Francesco Storace was Mayor.

164 Postal police, or Polizia postale: The branch of the police responsible for monitoring communications. The postal police investigate all crimes involving digital communications from fishing to frauds.

Clueless

Cavalette, A/I's blog, commented:

> These days, when all over Italy the police is complaining about reduced funds, we
> find it unexplainable that a private lawsuit filed at the Avezzano police office regarding
> minor events can unleash an international rogatory frenzy aimed at acquiring data
> that are inexistent and would be irrelevant to any investigation.
>
> We can explain this only if we assume that 'Casa Pound' has a certain influence in
> some sectors of the Italian police.[165]

Strengthening the idea that this enormous investigative effort was not matched by an equal
competency, there were a series of curious details from which it could be deduced that the
police forces were not capable of dealing with computer-related crime.

Firstly, given the letters of request, it was clear that they viewed A/I's statement as being neither
frank nor complete in so far as they declared to have neither the logs nor the personal details
related to the relevant mail account. But we know that this answer was not just honest – it's
a technical certainty.

Secondly, and a source of general hilarity, in the letter the name of the user and the domain
appeared in translation:

> [...] orsa@canaglie.net (she-bear@scoundrel.net) [...]

Both elements demonstrated scant competency in the technology through which the threats
mentioned in the request would have been made.

A doubt arose spontaneously that the reasons for this crackdown might be sought not on the
investigative but rather on the political level: of an order capable of setting into motion an
international legal apparatus, even with little hope of attaining anything and on the basis of
even less, if it were true that everything began with a slogan on a wall in Avezzano.

And at this point things took an unexpected turn. In civilized Norway – in contrast to what we
would have expected in Italy – the crackdown on A/I and resultant violation of its users' privacy
quickly took on the character of a full-blown scandal. A/I became famous and the case was
reported everywhere as emblematic of the pre-existing debate around data retention which
it is feared can be a means to restrict freedom of expression.

The newspaper headlines read: 'The police seized 7000 accounts just to save time'. And in
fact haste was the reason offered by the police initially to justify their actions in the court of
Norwegian public opinion, where they were accused of pursuing a vague foreign request for
information, and the seizure of an entire server of being unjustified and inexplicable.

---

165 Autistici/Inventati, 'Norwegian crackdown: fatti e note a margine', *Cavallette blog*, 22 November 2010,
     https://cavallette.noblogs.org/2010/11/7029.

How A/I Became a Media Cause Célèbre in Norway: The Datalagringsdirektivet Question

A/I's case was initially taken up by Jon Wessel-Aas of the Norwegian section of the International Commission of Jurists (ICJ). Wessel-Aas published a first article in which he reported on the affair. This article was quickly reprinted by others – the links are available on cavallette. noblogs.org – and then by the national radio morning news on NRK (the Norwegian state broadcaster).

The debate became more heated as the days passed: the Norwegians were indignant and complaints multiplied about the behavior of their own authorities. They also referred to the worrying socio-political situation in Italy. The A/I incident broke out right in the middle of the discussion on the *Datalagringsdirektivet* in Norway. The prospect of signing up to the European directive 2006/24/EF was raising many doubts and had already been the subject of lively arguments. The law would subsequently be approved on the 4 April 2011 by a small majority – eighty-nine in favor versus eighty against – and after nine hours of hard debate. The directive, already in force in Italy but rejected in Belgium and judged unconstitutional by Germany and Romania, obliges providers to retain data and is in conflict with Norwegian privacy law which lays down the exact opposite, namely the elimination of sensitive data.

Within the local political debate the subject was maddening: no-one appeared to want the law except for the government and the police force, who were running a public awareness campaign based on fighting terrorism and pedophilia.

The A/I case thus fit perfectly into this situation, even more so because although the debate was populated by many domestic issues, there was also an element of irritation at the excessive deference towards police in the EU (of which Norway is not part).

The behavior of the police was indicative of an acritical practice which the Norwegians would not forgive when the text of the letter of request ended up being printed in the papers: how is it possible that no-one demanded additional explanations from Italy before executing the order? In the Italian request there were neither reasons nor sufficient details to justify the alacrity with which the police saw fit to act.

The discussion continued on the *Datalagringsdirektivet* mailing list; there were some who adopted the position outlined by A/I's lawyer, according to whom the seizure was carried out in a manner inconsistent with the relevant legislation. The main arguments against the European Directive corresponded perfectly with A/I's complaints: in a democracy, it is citizens who control the state rather than the contrary. All citizens are innocent until proven guilty and not vice versa: the systematic monitoring of communications is in conflict with human rights.

Amongst the hardest and most authoritative positions was that taken in an official statement of IKT Norge (the trade association for the Norwegian computer industry) titled *The police demonstrate faulty judgment in the digital sector*.

Such unexpected exposure in the Norwegian media put the Norwegian police in difficulty. Following all this a fax response at last reached the Norwegian lawyer acting for the collective.

Answer to Questioning

The following are the words written by the Norwegian police in response to A/I and with which they explained their hasty *modus operandi*:

> I can assure you that the intent of the Norwegian police is to give as specific an answer to the request from the Italian authorities as possible. We are aware that the server contains a large amount of data that may not be relevant to the request, and this information will not be supplied to Italian authorities. Therefore, only the information that is relevant to the request from the Italian authorities, which concerns the mailbox music@autistici.org, will be included in the police report that will be prepared by the Norwegian police.

Music@autistici.org? The fax goes on:

> Regarding the mirroring of the hard disks, this method was chosen because the Norwegian service provider indicated to us that the data in question was deleted. That meant that the data had to be sought out and reconstructed – a process which our computer investigator says will take several weeks. The alternatives to mirroring the hard disks would have been seizing the disks or performing the investigation on the premises of the service provider. Both of these methods would have entailed disadvantages to the other, current users of the server, as well as economic disadvantages to the service provider. The choice of mirroring the entire hard disks do not, therefore, mean that it is the intent of the Norwegian authorities to transmit any data not related to music@autistici.org to Italian authorities, but is only the result of a wish to minimize the negative impact of our investigations.

The lawyer's next move was to ask for the return or destruction of the irrelevant data which had been copied. The *Ekomloven* was thus invoked, that is the set of rules which protect the users of information services against violations of the privacy agreements between users and service providers.

An agreement which had not actually been applied in the case of the disks' seizure because it stipulates a series of legal steps of which there was no trace in the documents provided to A/I.

And sure enough, predictably, the police's answer this time sounded a bit more bitter:

> The Police consider that neither Copyleft (the firm providing the co-location) nor Autistici/Inventati fall under the definition of service provider in the Communications Act. We are therefore of the opinion that the Criminal Procedure Act § 211 and § 212 does not apply in the current instance. For your information, some days ago the police learned that the Italian investigation which gave rise to the request had been dropped. Thus the analysis of the data contained on the disks has halted, pending clarification from the Italian authorities regarding the validity of the request. I have however today been informed that the Norwegian Post and Telecommunications Authority is processing a request from Autistici/Inventati to clarify whether Autistici/Inventati will be considered as service provider pursuant to Electronic Communications legislation. The Authority has indicated that they will give priority consideration to the case since clarification could have a bearing as to whether the seizure of those drives

was legitimate or not.[166]

Whilst awaiting further developments in this affair, greetings from planet Earth.

Toilet Duties by GINOX

I was raised with computers from an early age, like many of those born midway through the 70s. The VIC-20 and Commodore 64 were released when I was around eight. Like many of that generation I was brought up on TV movies, cartoons, and computers. I remember being fascinated by the imagery of awful TV series like *Whiz Kids* or *Riptide*, and recall an episode of *Simon & Simon* in which a young hacker, like the one in *War Games*, broke into a bank. Out of all this American trash I remember this rubbish specifically, and I believe this to be indicative of the fact that it affected my imagination.

In addition I was also a huge fan of the Edison twins. I don't know if that's a good or bad thing, but it's a fact. I've always been fascinated by laboratories, those enclosed gardens, *hortus conclusus*, where you focus yourself and shut everything else out. That must have been what it was like in the alchemist's closet. My interest has not been consistent over time: around fourteen or fifteen I was certainly maladjusted but not a PC nerd – computers had ceased to be of interest. Instead I had gotten into music, the punk and hardcore scene, and was fascinated by the mechanics of the self-managed spaces mainly because of their experimental nature, and whether this took social or technological form was a secondary consideration for me. If one really wants to draw a parallel the attitude is broadly similar: curiosity, the desire to take apart and reassemble the world, to make one's own decisions. And that, in my view, should be the purpose of every educational and pedagogical process, and is the only way to develop. I went to a Liceo Classico, a high school for humanities, and then studied history in university without getting a degree. Afterwards I returned to hacking for a series of reasons which could be described as political or existential.

In 1998, like many others, I was shaken by the affair involving Sole, Baleno, Silvano and Enrico.[167] Personally I came to a series of realizations. I sensed that the thread around which my life was spun – people, collectives, groups, and projects – was extremely fragile. Not because suicide must necessarily express fragility, quite the opposite: as far as I was concerned the problem was that our structures were so weak that individuals were forced into gestures both momentous and desperate. The unwilling protagonists of that affair were lynched in the media because we were incapable of countering the version propagated with a story of our own. Although we meant well, our resources and structures were completely inadequate, not just for a revolution but even for basic survival within a social context where you will be crushed as soon as there's money at stake. The high speed train corridor in the Susa Valley, and the whole story of the TAV in Italy, are symptomatic of this *modus operandi* and an interesting example of the paradigm of technology in the service of money. I won't repeat here

---

166 All quotes from a private communication between the Norwegian police and Autistici/Inventati's legal representatives.

167 Sole and Baleno: The two young anarchists who committed suicide in custody whilst under investigation for acts of sabotage on the high speed train system (TAV), for which they would be posthumously exonerated. Baleno killed himself in prison. Sole did the same some months later in a community where she was placed whilst awaiting trial. Silvano is the only one of those accused still alive. Enrico, president of the community and a friend of Sole, killed himself some months after her.

the arguments of those in Italy who have criticized the TAV, but I became interested again in technology and technics[168] during that period because our world was being built around it, and we were being crushed by it. Meaning was redefined solely to their benefit. Technics and technology needed first of all to be understood in their totality, as an ideology – because they are never neutral – but also had to be investigated practically. The last exams I sat in my history studies were those related to social anthropology, history of political doctrines, and moral philosophy. Then I transferred department and enrolled in computer science (which once again I didn't finish!). Not coming from an especially wealthy family, I had worked from twenty-one onwards and this, in addition to causing me much annoyance, provided me with firsthand experience and the stimulus to examine technology within productive and financial processes. My encounter with the Hackmeeting community took place in '98 at the first HackIT – the Italian Hackmeeting – in Florence, even if I didn't know any of those present. I knew no-one really until after HackIT in Rome in 2000, although I had hung around with all of them. Due to both shyness and a certain laziness I'm slow to become part of a group, moreover my 80s side left me with a love for 'plans which come together'. Thus I usually end up looking after logistical and technical matters. This element involves very little sociality; it's enough that everything functions correctly. I am a great fan of bathroom cleanliness; the people who I respect the most I have gotten to know cleaning the toilets. No one ever wants to clean the bogs because it's not a gratifying activity, but nonetheless they must be cleaned. Whoever cleans the bog thus confronts one of self-management's main problems. During that time I wondered to myself how I could contribute to the growth of a collective subject despite being someone who is quite solitary, bashful, not too accustomed to group work, and rather shaped by the philosophy of toilet duty.

To understand the meaning of the question you must consider that since adolescence I have been a lover of martial arts and combat sports. I have nurtured a deep fascination with some aspects of traditional Japanese culture; tripping out on that luxurious and vital artistic period which was Ukiyoe,[169] and the first time I saw the archival images of Zengakuren[170] occupying Shinjuku station I went through a wave of emotion, and indeed some sexual excitement, at their ability to move together, as one.

Now that the personality has been placed in context, let me try and illustrate my mental cogitations, which must be taken with a grain of salt. Or rather they should be taken as the words of a thirty-five year old who has half his body tattooed with tacky Japanese emblems and likes to roll about on the ground fighting, covering himself with cuts and scratches.

Judo has a motto which sounds positivistic, like something from days gone by, not at all postmodern and a touch simplistic. But this, I believe, is so that even kids can grasp it: Going Forward, Shining Together.

---

168 Technics: Here refers to the broad range of useful arts. Technology is understood as technique developed in the framework of industrialization.

169 Ukiyoe: A Japanese artistic movement at the turn of the 20th century. Usually it is presented as 'pictures of the floating world'. I really like an artist named Kuniyoshi who appears to have been somewhat flash and had a tattooed back. During this period, the Japanese tattoo as we imagine it today spread as a minor and somewhat extreme artistic form of Ukiyo-e. It was not tightly linked with the Yakuza, the Japanese Mafia, something which would happen only later after the Second World War.

170 The Zengakuren: Student movement in Japan around 1968. In October '68, in cooperation with some workers, they occupied Shinjuku station, a sort of symbol of westernized post-war Japan. Three days of street fights followed, then 1968 ended, 1969 began, and with it that void which is contemporary Japan.

It sounds like a slogan for a secular scout group, but in fact within judo instruction it has a pretty basic meaning. The capacity for growth as a group comes from the whole: not through the celebration of individuals in competition, nor from any vanguard, but indeed from everyone together. And it's only in this way that we grow individually; but at the same time every individual has their importance, because without them an experience would be missing, and it is through experience of practice that the group evolves. In judo all this has been distorted by competitiveness, which increases the ego and destroys the group to glorify the champion – but that's another story. To put it in anthropological terms it would be like saying that man is a symbolic animal determined by sociality. Not just a banal social animal, but one who processes symbols and lives inserted in a context. The nature of this context influences our capacity to develop within it. In a world where two thirds of humanity struggles for, or just doesn't get, the minimum to survive, the context is repellent and progress impossible. Analyzed through the pedagogical criteria of judo, we suck.

So that was more or less my idea when I got involved with A/I. A place like a dojo, a gym, in which one can get the skills to combine with experience. But also something more, a place in which sharing of knowledge takes place almost by osmosis, even if the subject is never posed directly, by virtue of the fact that there are others around you who use the same tools.

Starting from a structure dedicated ultimately to logistical and strategic tasks in the field of communication, and achieving something which enables cultural change and collective growth. Without loading meanings on it from on high, but rather allowing that meaning to emerge from the whole. I can't really put it any better than that, but I hope I've made myself clear.

I got to know A/I by hanging around those spaces in which the collective was founded: the hacklabs, Hackmeeting, and the self-managed spaces, around the year 2000. From my point of view the project had a relatively brief period of gestation; I joined the mailing list discussing its creation in September 2000 and by June 2001 it had already been publicly presented at the Hackmeeting in Catania.

A few weeks later we were in Genoa to set up the media center, and for me this exemplified the purpose of the project. Give energy to a movement, even if ridden with failings, strife and unceasing rows, because inside there were also people who were really worth it, and who drew from that humus the strength to live and grow, and in them there was the hope that the group could change and become stronger.

For me that's what some judo teachers called higher-level judo. The basic level is physical training, and even if it gets you to the Olympics it will always be limited. The higher level is the application of judo to life. Genoa was a huge defeat foretold, even if none of us expected to finish in a trap where the level of violence on the part of the security forces would be so high.

From a human point of view it was an extremely powerful experience, and for some a sort of pact sealed with tears, CS gas, blood, and wounds. But the movement didn't survive, individuals denied the group their strength exactly in the moment, perhaps, in which it was most needed, and after the parade of the Social Forum through Florence there was no longer the sensation that there existed something bigger, a whole.

This experience reinforced my conviction that the movement had been weak, and that it was necessary to create situations capable of providing at least a rock to which one could hold on so as not to be washed away by the waves. Realistically, A/I was not in a position to do more than that. That was the climax for me and has remained the gist of the project: grow when the movement grows, resist and be the rock when the movement explodes or implodes in on itself. So far it has worked, I think. In aikido you fall continuously, in judo as well – the first thing you are taught is to fall and get back up.

Fall and get back up. Fall and get back up.

Regarding the subsequent controversies and various crackdowns I don't know what to add which hasn't already been written in some communique. It's just the usual repression, which usually works out OK, we've never had really big problems. We perform a role which is not so easy to attack morally or ethically, and we are relatively old, don't panic on hearing the first bark, and have good lawyers.

Likewise as regards more recent history I don't have that much to say because I don't do that much in A/I any more. Because I can't stand spending so much time in front of the computer and am very focused on the age-old problem of cleaning the bog.

GLOSSARY

BBA (Big Brother Award). Is awarded to those who have been most damaging to people's privacy over the previous year and seeks to focus netizens' attention on those who contribute, actively or otherwise, to the threat to internet users' privacy. The prize is awarded in each country by different committees and each year has multiple categories including: 'Most Heinous Government', 'Worst Private Company', 'Most Appalling Project', 'Most Invasive Technology', and 'Lifetime Menace' going to whoever receives the most nominations for the award. There is also one category for people and organizations working to preserve or expand online privacy, the 'Winston Smith – Privacy Hero' award.

www.bigbrotherawards.org

www.bba.winstonsmith.org

BBS (Bulletin Board System). Developed at the end of the 1970s by Ward Christensen and Randy Suess, two students from the University of Chicago. In 1977 they wrote XMODEM, a program to transfer files from one computer to another. A year later BBcode was released, allowing the exchange of messages. Once installed, a BBS allows people to connect using a telephone line. The software allows users to exchange messages and files on the computer system. In the beginning, this system was very slow and not very widespread. Only after 1985, with the introduction of faster 1200 bps modems and the creation of large BBS networks, did it become widespread.

Besides some pioneers like AGHusa and CBBS, the first BBS network was FidoNet, which reached tens of thousands of nodes. However, great technical skills were required to manage a BBS, rendering it the domain of specialists and enthusiasts. With the introduction of the internet, BBS networks, although they still exist, were pretty much abandoned.

CA (Certification Authority or Certificate Authority). In cryptography, this is the trusted third party that releases digital certificates confirming that a public key (in the form of a certificate) belongs to the subject identified in that certificate. CA certificates authenticate a digital signature and fundamentally confirm that the website the user is accessing is really the one she was looking for. CAs release their certificates based on international standards, but must abide by the laws of their specific countries. This means that CAs exist and function in different ways depending on the specific local regulations. On the internet, cryptographic protocols use a public key infrastructure (PKI) based on a CA system to verify and confirm the identity of the parties. The goal of this infrastructure is to communicate without data being tampered with, forged or intercepted. Going up the chain of certificates in a PKI, you find one or more CAs (called Root CAs) which guarantee all the others. Root CAs are by necessity self-certified, with their guarantee ultimately being their good reputation. This is one of the reasons why today CAs are very important on the web, so much so that they are often run by multinational private bodies that sell certificates. However, there are several alternatives to commercial CA certificates, which can also be self-managed – written and signed by the organization that uses them, such as the ones used by the A/I collective until recently.

CHAINWORKERS. A group and an e-zine born in Milan inside the Bulk social center. Chainworkers first asked LOA, in 2000, to organize HTML courses for them to enable every contributor to publish directly in their new e-zine. In the following years Chainworkers developed into a collective focusing on precarity (the condition of casualized labour), launching Euro Mayday, San Precario – the patron saint of precarious workers – and the Serpica Naro 'designer label' and fashion show.

www.ecn.org/chainworkers/chainw/english.htm

CMS (Content Management System). A tool installed on a web server to simplify the management of web content by removing the need for administrators to have technical programming skills.

CC (Creative Commons). A kind of license inspired by the IT-related idea of copyleft. 'Copyleft', a play on the word 'copyright', was originally a label for free (as in speech) software, but it soon became a reference to the communities who embrace practices with the goal of establishing and spreading open source. To this end multiple licenses were created, including the GNU GPL, GNU LGPL, GFDL, etc. But unlike these, the CC licenses – which were invented by Lawrence Lessig and introduced in 2002 by the U.S. non-profit organization of the same name – are to be used for creative works. Based on the field of copyright, the CC licenses bypass the opposition between copyright (all rights reserved) and copyleft (no rights reserved) by offering the possibility to release content for free, but under certain conditions (some rights reserved). The author can give permission both to share her work (copy and distribute) and to create derivative works from it. The terms of use the licenses can require are: attribution (BY), non-commercial (NC), no derivative works (ND), and share alike (SA). The CC licenses are the result of the possible combinations of the terms of use, for instance: attribution (CC-BY), attribution non-commercial (CC-BY-NC), attribution no derivative works (CC-BY-ND), attribution share alike (CC-BY-SA), attribution non-commercial and no derivative works (CC-BY-NC-ND), attribution non-commercial and share alike (CC-BY-NC-SA). The CC licenses also allow for the author to renounce attribution (public domain, CC-0), but they do not include contradictory combinations (such as CC-BY-NC-ND-SA).

www.creativecommons.org

CRYPTOGRAPHY. Encryption is a system of encoding for content that allows for secure communication by stopping, more or less successfully, unauthorized people from accessing it. The most widespread system for encrypting e-mail messages is GNU Privacy Guard (GPG), the open-source that replaced PGP and offers the asymmetric encryption of messages. Thanks to a public key system, GPG creates sufficiently secure encryption, by allowing every user to disseminate their public key, which is used to encrypt messages that are then decoded with their private key. Another encryption system is TLS/SSL, a cryptographic protocol that forces all communication with a server into an 'encrypted channel' so that it cannot be tapped from outside. This mechanism requires the installation of a certificate (see CA) that enables the user's client to authenticate the server to establish an encrypted communication. Encryption via GPG is totally controlled by its users, while with TLS/SSL the server is responsible. However privacy-friendly the server admins may be, this system is therefore vulnerable in case of seizures to tampering and so on.

CYBER-RIGHTS. A pioneering mailing list focusing on rights related to communication and hosted by ECN, originally on their BBS and later on the web. Cyber-rights describes itself as an 'electronic, unmoderated public conference' discussing topics including copyright in multimedia works, public surveillance by new information technologies and social liberation movements' contribution to IT networks. As its editor (and not 'moderator'), Ferry Byte from the Strano Network group adds relevant materials to each debate.

www.ecn.org/cybr

DATA RETENTION, debate on. The retention of sensitive data defines the policies regarding the management of data flows, logging, and retention, with regards to legal requirements and economic interests. Data retention policies are based on the laws of the individual states. Nevertheless, what governments decide on the subject also depends on the global debate and frequently on specific international agreements. Issues concerning data retention raise both moral concerns for citizens (privacy), and economic concerns for providers. The current debate, which reflects both, has so far focused on two sets of issues: on the one hand, there is the question of how long is an acceptable retention period, what rules retention should follow and what formats should be used; on the other, there are the questions of retention methods, access and encryption.

DECODER. Biannual underground print magazine, created in Milan in 1986 and published until 1998 by the publishing house Shake Edizioni. It was one of the most important Italian reference points for cyberpunk culture, as this excerpt demonstrates:

> Some say CyberPunk is a fashion. On the contrary, we maintain that – to quote a famous definition of what should be "real" information – "CyberPunk is a difference which makes the difference". It has been a sensor and a push, towards the production of meaning, for ideas and real behaviors that, not long before, were adrift in their isolation and with no opportunity of landfall. By breaking the canon, a different imaginative horizon has been created, and new human relations and communities were born. With its process-oriented course, which re-elaborates information but considers information from the "inside", the CyberPunk attitude has challenged the categories of both "data" and "experience". The first issue was published in May 1987 and followed by eleven more. The magazine was a unique source of information on the Italian and international underground culture of the time, thanks to its columns, features and translations, as well as comics and book reviews. The Decoder group also launched a BBS of the same name. As early as the fifth issue, in July 1990, it voiced the need for an alternative computer network, summarizing the debate on computer activism that was taking place in social centers. The Decoder group got in touch with FidoNet through an administrator of the Milanese node and discussed the idea for a dedicated cyberpunk bulletin board. The project was launched in March 1991, with the creation of a discussion group that would soon become a hub for the exchange of information (and discussion) about hacking, computer networks, net art, new technologies and virtual realities. In 1993, the participants of the cyberpunk section of FidoNet, having reached a critical mass, launched a separate network, Cybernet, of which Decoder BBS was one of the four original nodes.[171]

Some issues of Decoder can be found on the Internet Archive (archive.org).

---

171 'Sommario', *Decoder* 8, Milano: Shake Edizioni Underground, 1993: 548.

ECN (European Counter Network). Over twenty years ECN gave voice to and hosted online Italian social centers, cultural associations, public spaces, trade unions, magazines, e-zines, underground radios – such as Radio Onda d'Urto in Brescia or Radio Black Out in Turin – and countless other projects. ECN allowed activists to create free information on diverse topics – from LGBTQ rights to the independent press. Thanks to ECN's long history, today these materials form an extensive archive of the Italian movement and its various parts.

One of the most interesting projects that arose from Isole nella Rete-ECN was Antifa, which monitored neofascist phenomena and antifascist activities in Italy. This initiative, as well as others, involved the ECN collective in several court cases. One case which is still famous is that of Giulio Caradonna, a former MP of the Movimento Sociale Italiano (Italian Social Movement – a neo- and post-fascist political party that merged in 1995 with conservative parts of Christian Democracy to form the National Alliance) who pressed charges against the association Isole nella Rete and the social center La Strada in 2000 with the aim of enforcing the 'right to be forgotten', by having information about him removed from an antifascist website. In 2004, ECN won at trial. For similar reasons, ECN has been literally repressed, for instance with the 1995 police raid at the Milanese social center Leoncavallo, where materials and equipment were vandalized, and the 1998 crackdown, which followed the first Hackmeeting in Florence by less than a month. In that instance, Paolo Pecori, the prosecutor of Vicenza, ordered the seizure of the server, which at the time was in Bologna, after a lawsuit for slander brought by Viaggi Turban Italia Srl, a firm based in Milan. The case revolved around the publication of a message containing information on the economic relationships between the agency and the former Turkish premier. The events were surrounded by a tense political climate, caused by the arrest in Italy and eventual extradition to Turkey of PKK leader Abdullah Öcalan. Nevertheless, not only did the message contain information that was widely known, but there was no apparent reason for ordering the seizure instead of demanding the removal of the relevant message. ECN's decade-long history is littered with similar events. Indeed Isole nella Rete was not only a radical organization defending free speech and the circulation of ideas – including prickly questions of copyright – but also ran an independent server that operated as part of a far broader discussion – the debate on digital rights and on the question concerning whether providers are responsible for the contents hosted in their servers. Many different powers and economic interests participate in this debate, from the governments, with their need to control, to the suppliers of big publishing companies.

www.ecn.org

EFF (The Electronic Frontier Foundation). An international non-profit digital rights group based in the United States. EFF fights for digital rights and freedom of speech in IT and in the world of communications more generally. Its main aim is to educate journalists, politicians and civil society about legislation concerning technology, as well as defend related freedoms. EFF offers and funds the legal defense of individuals and protects new technologies from 'chilling effect', i.e. restrictions on the exercise of rights deriving from fear of possible lawsuits; organizes political actions and mass mailings; fosters technologies that preserve personal freedoms; maintains a database and websites containing information on freedom of speech; monitors and challenges laws that may violate personal freedoms; and promotes the creation of lists of rights violations.

www.eff.org

FIDONET. In June 1984, Tom Jennings connected his and John Madill's BBSs giving birth to FidoNet, the first BBS network. After a year the network already had 160 nodes and began growing exponentially. With FidoNet, grassroots IT and hacking were born. For the first time, people exchanged information completely freely, at the grassroots level, fostered by the distribution mechanism itself, where the users were also the authors. It was not by chance that FidoNet's shared bulletin board was named 'anarchy' and the only requirement for participating was 'don't offend, and don't be too easily offended'. In Italy, FidoNet was born in 1986. In 1994, a police investigation on piracy and child pornography online started by prosecutors in Turin and Pesaro led to the simultaneous seizure of dozens of BBS nodes connected to FidoNet, with very serious consequences. These events, which took place on the 11 May, would become known as the Italian Crackdown. Contrary to the media's predictions during their long smear campaign against computer hobbyists, the investigation ended without any prosecutions. Eventually the court concluded that FidoNet had not been implicated in the exchange of pirated software. In Italy, on this sorrowful note, the era of BBSs ended and that of the internet began.

FILE SHARING. A practice in which users move files from one computer to another via programs that use peer-to-peer (P2P) networks or client-server architectures. File sharing has become popular with the spread of broadband internet access. The practice arose with BBS networks, which already had an area for exchanging files, and it developed as digital tools became widespread and easier to use. The most significant events that brought file sharing to its current level were the development of MP3, the format that made audio files smaller and therefore easier to share, and the launch of Napster, file sharing software conceived by Shawn Fanning and Sean Parker in 1999. Napster made the practices of file sharing known all over the world and is still famous not only because of the tool itself, but because the major record companies pressed charges against its creator, who was eventually found guilty. Since then things have changed, and in fact many trials have ended with the confirmation of the legal innocence of peer-to-peer practices and, above all, have limited the responsibilities of the developers of file sharing software. The Supreme Court of the United States, for instance, has stated that P2P is only a criminal practice if the software inventor's intention is clearly to infringe upon copyright laws. Among the victories and defeats in court, political battles against copyright, ethical questions around free sharing of material and all the other things that took place in the universe of file sharing, it is worth noting that over the years many artists – the main actors of copyright protection – have embraced P2P, denying the alleged economic damage to the recording industry, and embracing it as a useful way to distribute their art and, thus, a source of publicity.

FLUG (Firenze Linux User Group). Linux Users Groups (LUGs) are organizations of Linux users working in their local area. They usually have the Italian Linux Society (ILS), as their point of reference, but are independent from it. Like other LUGs, the FLUG focuses on spreading and developing free software and is open to everyone who wishes to cooperate with it, as long as they respect its manifesto. In general, the group's aim is to distribute software that does not force users to use a program in a certain way, and the organization's favorite operating system is Linux 'because Linux derives its technical force from being a UNIX operating system and its ethical power from being FREE'. More specifically, the FLUG creates software, documentation, and translations that are all released under free licenses. From 1998 to 2008, the FLUG regularly organized courses for getting acquainted with 'the penguin's operating system'. Since March 2009, it has organized random meetings on a single topic along the hacknight scheme, and the Linux Day in Florence. In 2003, the FLUG connected a server, the 'serverone', or 'big server', to the web in order to host services for its community and for similar groups based in other cities. On the 27 June 2005, the FLUG noticed that its server, hosted in the Milanese headquarters of Inet, a provider, had been physically compromised. The server did not contain any sensitive data, apart from that necessary for managing the services and a few FLUG members' private mailboxes. A new installation was carried out from scratch on the server, and went back online on the 3 August 2005.

www.firenze.linux.it

FREAKNET. Founded in Catania as a BBS network disconnected from the FidoNet global circuit, with the aim of being a genuinely free network, 'politically akin to, but methodologically different from the networks of Cybernet and ECN'. In Freaknet, Asbesto, and Hecatombles met Shining, who worked with *I Siciliani*, a magazine published on the network which became the first publication with a digital edition in Italy. The Freaknet group asked for and obtained a room in the Auro social center in Catania. There they set up the MediaLab, the first lab dedicated to free technology in Italy, made almost entirely out of donated hardware and pieces of old computers literally saved from landfills and dumpsters. For years, the Freaknet MediaLab offered, for free, a digital service that was unique in Italy: open, unsurveilled access to its users, where their data was stored and discreetly protected against any deletion or change, accidental or otherwise. Copies of the data were made regularly, and these copies were kept in secret, inaccessible places by trusted people, who did not know anything about the content of these backups to ensure their security (especially from abuses of power). The members of Freaknet also studied thoroughly how to keep their computer network safe from viruses and attacks, so much so that the Freaknet MediaLab never suffered a serious malfunction.

Beginning in 1999, the MediaLab offered about 15 introductory computer courses. In 2001, the Auro social center and the Freaknet MediaLab hosted a Hackmeeting, from the 22 to the 24 June, where 'the main highlight was neither technology, nor politics, mixed in equal parts, but the community and the strengthening of relationships'. When the social center was evicted, all activity there stopped and the MediaLab was temporarily hosted in the Poetry Hacklab in the village of Palazzolo Acreide. Over the years, Freaknet has collected hundreds of computer manuals, operating systems, applications, and components, as well as a wide range of disks of various dimensions, mostly containing software and drivers for DOS from the past. Furthermore, several of its old computers have been cataloged and restored in order to create the Museum of Functioning IT.

www.freaknet.org

www.museo.freaknet.org/en

FTP. File transfer protocol, it is a method for the uploading and downloading of files between a client (user's computer) and a server (machine hosting files online).

G8 GENOA, 20-22 July 2001. The 27th G8 international summit was held in Genoa, Italy. As happened during similar events, the anti-globalization movement organized a counter-summit, with several marches and a final demonstration. But unlike those other instances, in Genoa the unthinkable happened: Carlo Giuliani, a young protester, was killed. The counter-summit became sadly famous for the police violence during the demonstrations on Friday 21 and Saturday 22 July. The violence reached its peak Saturday evening during the raid on the Diaz school and continued the following days in the Bolzaneto police barracks.

GPG (GNU Privacy Guard). See PGP.

GPL (General Public License). GNU GPL, or more simply GPL, is the most widely used free software license. It was written originally by Richard Stallman for the GNU project.

www.gnu.org/copyleft/gpl.html

HACKMEETING. The annual meeting of the Italian digital counterculture. The Hackmeeting is attended by 'groups and individuals who have a critical and proactive attitude towards new technology'. Fundamentally, the Hackmeeting consists of three days of workshops, debates, exchanges of opinions, collective learning, games, and parties and is traditionally hosted by self-managed spaces such as social centers and squats. The first Hackmeeting was held from the 5 to the 7 June 1998 in Florence, at the social center Centro Popolare Autogestito Firenze Sud (CPA), and was in part a response to the changed climate for hackers after the Italian Crackdown of 1994, which marked the beginning of legal proceedings against computer hobbyists. At the time, members of FidoNet were indicted for conspiracy, smuggling, duplicating software, and intrusion into third-party computer systems. Even as these accusations turned out to be groundless, FidoNet was dismantled, and any attempt at understanding the logic of new technologies was dismissed by the media as a sort of 'new criminal phenomenon'. The first Hackmeeting was organized by ECN, Decoder from Milan, AvANa BBS from Rome, Freaknet from Catania, Metro Olografix from Pescara, CyberNet and, of course, the CPA Hacklab from Florence together with Strano Network.

Since then, the meeting has been organized by hackers and activists fighting for digital freedom, using a mailing list currently hosted by A/I as a tool for coordination. Everyone can help plan and create the event, as well as suggest workshops and conferences.

Not one year has passed without hackers, nerds, curious people, activists, and more meeting to discuss what is happening around them and to practically demonstrate that any tool (from PCs to media) can be manipulated in order to turn it into something different, better and most of all free from the logic of hierarchy and power. In the following years, the Hackmeeting has been held in Milan (1999), Rome (2000), Catania (2001), Bologna (2002), Turin (2003), Genoa (2004), Naples (2005), Parma (2006), Pisa (2007), Palermo (2008), Milan (2009), Rome (2010), Florence (2011), L'Aquila (2012), Cosenza (2013), Bologna (2014), Napoli (2015), Pisa (2016).

www.hackmeeting.org

INDIVIA. Born from the need for virtual space for projects with the purpose of sharing knowledge and experiences, Indivia aims to become a first node in a server that is closer to the concept of network. It aims to be more modular, collective, scalable, and with a structure capable of incorporating other nodes in a perspective that refuses the typical singular machine bestowing services.

www.indivia.net

JABBER. A communication protocol used for instant messaging that was developed in 1999 by the open-source community of the same name. This protocol, which is also used for voice over IP (VoIP) technology, is currently referred to as XMPP. Unlike most instant messaging tools, Jabber has an open approach to both its development and implementation. This means that anybody can offer a Jabber service that is interoperable with similar services. Many clients using this protocol are available as open source and free software. A/I chose to offer Jabber because these features make it a good basis for secure communication and because communications via Jabber can be encrypted with a system called OTR.

https://www.autistici.org/docs/jabber/

KRIPTONITE. The collective work of a certain part of the Italian IT counterculture detailing the risks of surveillance on the web and possible solutions. The book, *Kriptonite. Fuga dal controllo globale. Crittografia, anonimato e privacy nelle reti telematiche* (*Kryptonite. Escape from Global Control. Cryptography, Anonymity and Privacy on Computer Networks*) by Joe Lametta was published in 1998 by the independent publisher Nautilus in Turin under the pen name Joe Razor Blade. The book was released without copyright and is available in its entirety online.

www.ecn.org/kriptonite

LOGS. See No-Logs.

MIRROR. The copy of a website made available on a separate party's server. Mirrors are often created by supporters of a threatened website where there is a risk of the original being closed down by legal action or direct technological attack (as is the case with a distributed denial of service attack, or DDOS, similar to a netstrike).

MOLLEINDUSTRIA. A producer of free, short-form, online games that have offered homeo-pathic remedies to the idiocy of mainstream entertainment in the form since 2003. Molleindu-stria products range from satirical business simulations (*McDonald's Video game, Oiligarchy*) to meditations on labor and alienation (*Every Day the Same Dream, Tuboflex, Unmanned*) and from playable theories (the *Free Culture Game, Leaky World*) to politically incorrect games (*Orgasm Simulator, Operation: Pedopriest*).

www.molleindustria.org

NO-LOGS. A mechanism that creates obstacles for an entity trying to trace a user on the internet, this term could be a good synthesis for A/I's approach. Today, Western societies are making huge regulatory – and therefore technological – efforts to connect virtual actions to the physical person from which they originate (see data retention). Despite it being tech-nically possible to trace the owner of a telephone line (which doesn't have to be the person using it), the structure of the web makes it difficult to find information about the person who carried out a single action on the internet, because tracking the route of data is complicated. However, communications between computers leave signs – called logs – which can be recorded by the servers and used to trace the user. Essentially, Autistici amplifies noise on the internet by creating a further obstacle for those who may be interested in monitoring a user. The same mechanism that allows for identification – the possibility of checking logs – is removed. 'No-logs' does not refer to a technology, but to its absence. Providers have always voluntarily kept logs as long as they are needed for problem solving (e.g. in case e-mails are lost). Today, due to the aforementioned efforts, logs are retained much longer than needed, for the purpose of profiling users. While in the past an attempt to track a sender might not have been successful, today it undoubtedly would succeed. A/I does not keep any logs. Looking constantly for a balance between the usefulness of logs in problem solving and their risks to users' anonymity, A/I keeps track of the traffic in its servers only when absolutely necessary in the provision of a service. These are 'limited' logs – partial data without any connection to the user's identity. A/I does not delete data: very simply, data is never generated. This is one of the reasons why A/I's servers are hosted in countries where data retention is not mandatory. For the collective, helping to protect users' anonymity on the web is working to maintain the original nature of the internet, when every computer was equal and freedom of speech was in its heyday.

NYMWARS. Conflicts over policies requiring users of internet services to identify themselves using legal names. This term was coined in July 2011 with the launch of Google+ and the introduction of its new policy.

ORANGE BOOK. The document published by the A/I Collective in 2004, detailing the reflections that led to Plan R* and its technical structure.

www.autistici.org/orangebook

OZIOSI. A term that acknowledges laziness, slowness and idleness as a natural condition towards which men and women aspire. Oziosi.org offers mailboxes, mailing lists, galleries and a wiki, and organizes the Perugia Free Media Days, an event which explores the world and alternative solutions of communication.

www.oziosi.org

P2P. See File sharing.

PACKET ANALYZER. A packet analyzer (also known as a network analyzer, protocol analyzer or packet sniffer, or, for particular types of networks, an Ethernet sniffer or wireless sniffer) is a computer program or a piece of computer hardware that can intercept and log traffic passing over a digital network or part of a network. These programs can be used for purposes both legitimate (i.e. for traffic analysis, to identify communications problems or intrusion attempts) and illegitimate (i.e. the fraudulent tapping of sensitive data). In order to tap data in a local network, physical access is needed. The way to defend against such an attack is through the encryption of traffic.

PGP (Pretty Good Privacy). Free encryption software developed by Phil Zimmermann in 1991. Zimmermann was an anti-nuclear activist who created PGP in order to give his comrades security as they used BBSs, storing messages and files. He published the source code using a common right formula which didn't require users to buy a license unless they wanted to use the software for commercial purposes. PGP spread quickly on Usenet and the internet. The diffusion of PGP was strongly hampered by the American government, and the legal vicissitudes Zimmerman faced were terrible. PGP is a public-key encryption program developed to solve a classical paradox of cryptography – the use of a single key for encryption and decryption. Instead, PGP is based on two keys: a public and a private key. The public key is only used to encode the message, whereas the secret key only decodes it. Metaphorically speaking, the message bounces twice between the sender and the receiver before the latter can read it, but they don't need to exchange the key. Essentially, PGP abolishes the weak spot of every cryptographic strategy – the moment when the two parties in the relationship must exchange the key 'in plain text' (i.e. without encryption). Every PGP user creates her key pair.

The private key must be kept secret, while the public key is disseminated and made available to everyone who wants to communicate with the user. Generally, public keys are stored in public archives (called keyservers) and are available to anybody who wishes to download them.

Among encryption systems, PGP is considered one of the most reliable. Even if it is mostly used to protect e-mails, which don't have a native security system, PGP can be used to protect any kind of file, data or backup.

PLAN R*. A reference to Dr. Strangelove as well as a *détournement* of the Masonic lodge P2 (Licio Gelli's 'Plan for Democratic Rebirth'), Plan R* is A/I's response to a series of technical weaknesses, whose worst consequence was the Aruba crackdown. At the same time, Plan R* is a long-term strategy conceived to protect the project as a whole from the wave of repression that followed the 2001 G8 summit in Genoa. The name Plan R* refers to concepts such the Resilience (of the project), the Resistance (against the authorities' attacks), and the Revolution (of the infrastructure). The analysis and motives of Plan R* are described in the Orange Book, with an extensive documentation of its architectural and technical features.

> As early as in 2003, the collective began to foresee the coming wave of repression and imagine its possible forms. At the time we thought that the growing importance of digital communication tools, especially within radical political contexts, would soon be targeted by the forces of repression. We had been optimistic: since then we have seen a growing global paranoia give new drive to the Orwellian and Panoptical ideologies of total control, that now target not only the limited groups of protesters, but the whole society. Plan R* was developed over a period of two years. A/I first identified its weak spots: the servers were being hosted either by a commercial provider or in houses and social centers where physical defense was unrealistic; there was a concentration in one server of too much personal data and a lack of a widespread culture of digital self-defense among users; the legal landscape had evolved, leading to a multiplication of hardware seizures. Later, after having negotiated a series of ideas that had meanwhile become less sustainable, the collective transitioned to the new infrastructure. When it was implemented, in October 2005, Plan R* turned out to be a complicated operation of decentralization, aiming at increasing the cost and complexity of seizures to the point of making them unfeasible, by multiplying and blurring the attack surface across many subjects in different nations with different regulations.[172]

> https://www.autistici.org/who/rplan/intro

PRAGUE, 2000. International counter-summit and demonstrations that were organized on the 26-30 September 2000 to protest against the World Bank and International Monetary Fund meetings in Prague. With its violent clashes in the streets, this was the first European meeting for the anti-globalization movement after the great hype generated by the international protests in Seattle in December 1999 (N30, or 'Battle of Seattle'), which is widely considered the birthplace of the anti-globalization movement (also called the 'People of Seattle').

In Seattle, protesters had made the difference – not only did they virtually block the WTO summit they were protesting against, they also stood out as a successful international coordination, for the lack of divisions among the demonstrators, for the deep understanding of

---

172 Autistici/Inventati, 'Introduction', *Orange Book*, https://www.autistici.org/orangebook.

the issues raised by the protests, for the use of the internet to manage contacts, and for Indymedia's real-time coverage of events. In Prague, during the international demonstration, protesters were divided into three different groups advancing from three different directions to the conference center where the talks were taking place. The yellow block performed actions inspired by civil disobedience; the pink block advanced through what they called 'tactical frivolity', with music, dances, and theater performances. The blue block clashed directly with the police, mostly by throwing cobblestones, but there were some unforgettable incendiary incidents too. Between Seattle 1999 and Genoa 2001, the European events that brought the anti-globalization movement together were: Nice, France (December 2000, meeting of the European Council); Davos, Switzerland (World Economic Forum, January 2001); Naples, Italy (March 2001, OECD Global Forum on E-goverment); Gothenburg, Sweden (June 2001, meeting of the European Council); Barcelona, Spain (June 2001, ABCDE, cancelled); Salzburg, Austria (July 2001, World Economic Forum).

PRIX ARS ELECTRONICA. Annual prize dedicated to digital art, computer animation, and interactive arts, and music. Since 1987, it has been presented during the Ars Electronica Festival in Linz, Austria. Winners receive a small golden reproduction of the Nike of Samothrace. The Prix Ars Electronica, the Ars Electronica Festival, the Ars Electronica Center-Museum of the Future, and the Ars Electronica Futurelab are the four divisions of Ars Electronica Linz GmbH, which has established itself as one of the main organizations promoting this kind of art and culture.

www.aec.at

RISEUP. An autonomous body based in Seattle with collective members worldwide. Like A/I in Italy, the Riseup collective considers it vital that essential communication infrastructures are not controlled by companies and authorities, but by the movement. Therefore the group aims to keep its users' e-mail as safe and private as possible. Riseup's purpose is to aid in the creation of a free society, a world with freedom from want and freedom of expression, a world without oppression or hierarchy, where power is equally shared. They do this by providing communication and computer resources to allies engaged in struggles against capitalism and other forms of oppression.

www.riseup.net

RSS. Really simple syndication, a collection of standards for web feeds. This allows updated information from one website to be published in headline form on another site or sent to a client application called an RSS reader. RSS obviates the need for a user to actively visit the originating website in order to view its most recent publications.

SERPICA NARO. Anagram of San Precario, the patron saint of precarious workers, Serpica Naro made its first exploit in 2005, when it became well known all over Italy. On the 26 February 2005, passing themselves off as a young Anglo-Japanese artist and designer, Serpica Naro, the collective behind San Precario managed to take part in the final day of Milan Fashion Week. On that day journalists and fashion workers flocked into the tent built by reLOAd near the Pergola social center in Milan to watch the fashion show of precarious work. Shouting 'we are not low class, we are not high class, we are the new class', eight models 'sarcastically representing some aspects of precarious life' walked down the catwalk; clothes which conceal pregnancy so as not to be fired; anti-groping skirts full of rat traps; sexy mini-skirts for a faster career; bridal dresses for women without Italian citizenship, as the only way to get it is to marry an Italian man; overalls hiding pajamas, to always be ready to work, even at night; reversible suits for those who have two jobs; anti-stress clothes against exhaustion, and T-shirts with the number of days before you get fired. Then finally, some 'genuine productions by the precarious textile designers who disdain the fashion mainstream': a series of models of DIY products.

In the following years, Serpica became a meta-brand, the first brand released under a Creative Commons license that can be used by all those who don't exploit employees and precarious workers.

www.serpicanaro.com

SNIFFER. See Packet Analyzer.

SOCIAL NETWORKS. Services whereby individuals can create a user profile and then construct a web of relations with other users. This web can then function as a conduit for the circulation of messages and media between users, with a group, or the public at large. These services can be centralized or federated. In the former case all the information passes through a central server infrastructure owned by a corporation (Facebook, Twitter). Federated social networks use a common protocol to allow independently operated systems to interact with one another and provide the same functionality, Diaspora is an example.

STRANO NETWORK. Today Strano Network is a cultural association organizing events focused on arts and new communication tools. It was established in Florence in 1993 to maintain a 'permanent workshop for multimedia countercultural communication' at the Ex-Emerson social center in Florence as well as Hacker Art BBS, one of the first four nodes of the Cybernet network. In 1994, based on an idea by Prof. Tommaso Tozzi – now director of the Department of Multimedia Arts, as well as professor at the Academy of Fine Arts of Florence and Carrara and president of Strano Network – the group launched a new BBS system, Virtual Town Television, a memorable Florentine database.

Among Strano Network's various initiatives related to the hacker community and activism, it is worth recalling the 1996 'net strike' against the US judiciary (and for Mumia Abu Jamal and Silvia Baraldini) – a DDoS attack that blocked the White House website for twelve hours – and the organization of the first Hackmeeting, which took place in Florence in 1998. Over the years, Strano Network has encouraged reflection on arts and networks, on the use and abuse of communications, copyright, and social hacking. The group has also organized happenings with electronic music, virtual reality installations, and ironic exhibitions on the changes in Western costumes.

www.strano.net

SSL CERTIFICATES, or **Secure Sockets Layer**. The old name for transport layer security (TLS). This is a cryptographic protocol that enables a client and server to communicate with one another securely. The website uses a certificate signed by a reputable third party to establish its identity. This certificate is actually a public key and linked to a private counterpart. This use of key pairs is referred to as asymmetric cryptography and relies upon a public key infrastructure where trusted third parties endorse keys of reputable users. Once contact is established in this way, one-time keys are exchanged and are used to secure all subsequent communication.

TEKNUSI. A collective formed by individuals who were mostly from Southern Italy but are now scattered around the world. Teknusi.org (ca. 2003-2011) was born as a sort of technical 'training ground' for other projects, as well as a home-made server offering services ensuring anonymity, privacy, and a proper idea of security. Through the years, the teknusi.org collective dedicated most of its energies to icecast streaming and helping many small and large grassroots activist radios.

TOR (originally The Onion Router). Free software for enabling online anonymity based on the second generation of the onion routing protocol. Tor protects users from traffic analysis through a network of onion routers (also called relays) managed by volunteers. This network makes outgoing traffic anonymous and makes it possible to create anonymous hidden services. Originally sponsored by the US Naval Research Laboratory, Tor was a project of the Electronic Frontier Foundation and is now run by The Tor Project, a non-profit organization.

www.torproject.org

USENET. A contraction of the words 'user' and 'net', Usenet is a communication system based on a 'computer network' – a worldwide server network formed by thousands of connected computers. Its purpose is to gather and organize, in a publicly accessible archive, the messages, information, and content that the people who can access the servers send each other in form of 'news' (so various topical areas are called 'newsgroups'). Usenet, an internet service, was invented in 1979 and implemented in 1980 by two students at Duke University, Tom Truscott and Jim Ellis, and is still widely used. It has played a very important role in the history of IT. For example, it was within Usenet that terms like 'spam' and 'FAQ' were coined. Usenet is akin to the BBSs, but its interactions are midway between an e-mail service and a web forum.

WEB FARM. A web farm aka server farm aka co-location facility offers hosting facilities to site operators, either on their own servers or through the installation of a server on their premises, which are often designed for security and equipped with high-speed connections to the internet backbone.

References

Agnoletto, Vittorio. 'Diritto alla "privacy" e abusi nei confronti degli "utenti internet" di "INVESTICI"', question before the European Parliament, 12 July 2005, https://www.autistici.org/ai/crackdown/stampa/interrogazione_parlamento_europeo.

Autistici/Inventati. 'Introduction', *Orange Book*, https://www.autistici.org/orangebook.

Autistici/Inventati. 'God Bless America", *Cavallette blog*, 4 July 2007, https://cavallette.noblogs.org/2007/07/641.

Autistici/Inventati. 'Norwegian crackdown: fatti e note a margine', *Cavallette blog*, 22 November 2010, https://cavallette.noblogs.org/2010/11/7029.

backbone409 organizers. 'Backbone409: Participants', 2014, https://backbone409.calafou.org.

Bazzichelli, Tatiana. *Networking: The Net as Artwork*, Aarhus: Digital Aesthetics Research Center, Aarhus University, 2009.

Big Brother Award Italia, 2008, http://bba.winstonsmith.info/bbai2008html.

Bre and Astera (eds) *Hackerspaces: The Beginning*, 2008. Available at: http://blog.hackerspaces.org/2011/08/31/hackerspaces-the-beginning-the-book/.

Coleman, Gabriella and Golub, Alex. 'Hacker Practice: Moral Genres and the Cultural Articulation of Liberalism', *Anthropological Theory* 8.3 (September, 2008): 255-277.

Collettivo NGN, *Mela Marcia*, Milano: Agenzia X, 2010.

Court of Milan, appeal verdict on Associazione Investici vs. Trenitalia SpA case, https://www.autistici.org/ai/trenitalia/documenti/5_sentenza_ricorso.

darkveggy. 'Invitation to "Connect Congress 2004" in BCN', posting to the hacklabs mailing list, 13 October 2004, https://listas.sindominio.net/pipermail/hacklabs/2004-October/000608.html.

Di Corinto, Arturo and Tozzi, Tommaso. *Hacktivism: La libertà nelle maglie della rete*, Roma: Manifestolibri, 2002, www.hackerart.org/storia/hacktivism.htm.

Hardt, Michael. 'Introduction: Laboratory Italy', in Michael Hardt and Paolo Virno (eds) *Radical Thought in Italy: A Potential Politics*, Minnesota: University of Minnesota Press, 1996, 1-10.

Kulla, Daniel. *Der Phrasenprüfer: Szenen aus dem Leben von Wau Holland, Mitbegründer des Chaos-Computer-Clubs* [the Voltage Tester – Scenes from the Life of Wau Holland, Co-Founder of the Chaos Computer Club], Birkenau-Löhrbach: Werner Pieper & The Grüne Kraft, 2003.

Lametta, Joe. *Kriptonite. Fuga dal controllo globale. Crittografia, anonimato e privacy nelle reti telematiche*, Torino: Nautilus, 1998, http://www.nautilus-autoproduzioni.org/wp-content/uploads/2015/01/KRIPTO.pdf.

Levy, Steven. *Hackers: Heroes of the Computer Revolution*, Garden City, NY: Anchor Press, Doubleday, 1984.

Maxigas. *Peer Production of Open Hardware: Unfinished Artefacts and Architectures in the Hackerspaces*, PhD diss., Barcelona: Internet Interdisciplinary Institute/Open University of Catalunya, 2015.

Molleindustria. 'Operation: Pedopriest', website and video game, 2007, www.molleindustria.org/en/operation-pedopriest.

Montaparadiso Hacklab wiki contributors. 'Transnational Hackmeeting', 2004, http://web.archive.org/web/20040607030557/http://twiki.fazan.org/bin/view/Transhackmeeting.

'Sommario', *Decoder* 8, Milano: Shake Edizioni Underground, 1993: 548-550.

Subcomandante Marcos, 'Statement of Subcomandante Marcos to the Freeing the Media Teach-In', 31 January/1 February 1997, https://www.tmcrew.org/chiapas/e_media1.htm.

SupportoLegale. 'Comunicato di SupportoLegale', *Autistici*, June 2005, https://www.autistici.org/ai/crackdown/comunicati/comunicato_supporto_legale.

Tamás, Polgár. *Freax: The History of the Computer Demoscene*, Winnenden: CSW-Verlag, 2005.

transhackmeeting.org. '(Un)hack the Bosphorus: TransHackMeeting Istanbul 2010', Slides from the HackerSpaceFestival, /tmp/lab near Paris, France, 2009, http://sandbox.benn.org/sli/hsf2009/thk2010_hsf2009.pdf.

Turner, Fred. *From Counterculture to Cyberculture: Stewart Brand, the Whole Earth Network, and the Rise of Digital Utopianism*, Chicago, IL: University of Chicago Press, 2006.

United Nations Office on Drugs and Crime, 'Database of Legislation: Italy', https://www.unodc.org/cld/en/legislation/ita/codice_penale/libro_secondo/articles_600-600septies2/article_600ter-600septies2.html?.

Velena, Helena. Talk at 'Diritto alla comunicazione nello scenario di fine millennio – Iniziativa nazionale in difesa della telematica amatoriale', conference organized by Strano Network, Centro per l'Arte Contemporanea Luigi Pecci, 19 February 1995, Prato, http://www.strano.net/snhtml/atticonv/velena.htm.

ZERO! and BITs Against The Empire Labs (eds). *Digital Guerrilla. Guida all'uso alternativo di computer, modem e reti telematiche,* 1995, www.ecn.org/zero/digguer.htm.

www.ingramcontent.com/pod-product-compliance
Lightning Source LLC
LaVergne TN
LVHW012331060326
832902LV00011B/1829